The Tibetan Book of the Dead

A Comprehensive Summary, Guidebook and Modern Day Exploration for Beginners and Seasoned Buddhists

Lobsang Tenzin Dorje

Contents

Introduction & Structure of the Tibetan Book of the Dead

Embracing the Cycle of Existence

At the heart of the vast Tibetan plateau, a text was conceived over a millennium ago that continues to captivate the spiritual and curious minds of today: "The Tibetan Book of the Dead" or "Bardo Thödol." This ancient manuscript, traditionally believed to be the teachings of Padmasambhava, an 8th-century master, has guided countless souls through the intricate journey between death and rebirth. Its origins steeped in mystery and tradition, it emerged as a beacon for those seeking to understand the transient nature of life and the grandeur of what lies beyond.

Life, death, and rebirth - these aren't just cycles in a bestselling fantasy novel. They are the very core of our existence. Now, you might be thinking, "But I'm not a Tibetan monk, why should I care?" Well, dear reader, that's the magic of this journey. Whether you're a seasoned Buddhist practitioner or someone who just stumbled upon this book because it looked intriguing, the wisdom that unfolds within these pages is universal.

The Tibetan Book of the Dead, contrary to what its title might suggest, isn't just about the afterlife. It offers us a mirror to our souls, a guide to navigate the intricate maze of our emotions, and a compass that points towards the true nature of existence. But, wait, don't just take my word for it. By the end of this book, you'll see for yourself!

The teachings of the Bardo resonate beyond geographical and religious boundaries, embodying truths that are profoundly human and universally applicable. Every soul, whether consciously or unconsciously, is on a quest to unravel the mysteries of existence. This comprehensive summary and guidebook is designed to offer insights, reflections, and practices that are pertinent to every stage of your spiritual journey. The wisdom within these pages promises to enlighten the mind, enrich the soul, and guide seekers on a transformative path of discovery and awakening.

Imagine embarking on an exploration depicted as a rich tapestry, interwoven with threads of ancient wisdom, contemporary interpretations, and your own unique experiences. Together, we will delve deeply into its teachings, tracing the origins and influences of the text, and exploring its impact on both Eastern and Western shores. We will navigate through the Bardos, those intricate realms that exist between life and rebirth, armed with practices that guide us through their complexities. Each chapter, each page, serves as an invitation to pause, reflect, and immerse oneself in these profound teachings, illuminating our path with enduring insights and timeless wisdom.

So, with an open heart, an inquisitive mind, and perhaps a cup of your favorite brew, let's set sail on this enlightening adventure. May this exploration serve not just as a study of an ancient text but as a transformative experience, reinvigorating your perspective on the world, death, and life with newfound clarity and wisdom.

The Concept of the Bardo

In Tibetan Buddhism, the concept of the Bardo plays a pivotal role, acting as a bridge between life, death, and rebirth. The term 'Bardo,' translating to 'intermediate state' or 'transitional state,' offers profound insights into the nature of existence and consciousness. This chapter unfolds the multi-layered understanding of the Bardo, exploring its various stages and the wisdom it holds for both the transient and the eternal.

At its core, the Bardo represents the transitional phases between different states of existence. It's not merely a passageway between life and death but a mirror reflecting the depth and breadth of consciousness. In Tibetan Buddhism, the Bardo is seen as a crucial opportunity for spiritual realization and liberation, a time where the mind is unbound by the physical body, offering a unique perspective on the true nature of reality.

The Bardo is both a state of being and a journey, a landscape of the mind where one's deepest fears and greatest potentials are revealed. It is a space where the duality of existence is magnified, where illusions are stripped away, revealing the luminous nature of mind and the interconnectedness of all beings.

The journey through the Bardo is marked by various stages and transitions, each with its characteristics and lessons. The Tibetan Book of the Dead outlines six Bardos: three of them are related to our earthly existence (Kyenay Bardo, Milam Bardo, and Samten Bardo), and the other three are connected to the dying process and after-death experiences (Chikhai Bardo, Chonyi Bardo, and Sidpa Bardo).

Each stage of the Bardo offers different opportunities and challenges, guiding the individual towards self-realization and enlightenment. The transitions between these stages are times of profound transformation, where the individual confronts their karma, makes choices that influence their rebirth, and potentially attains liberation from the cycle of samsara.

Traversing through the Bardos requires mindfulness, wisdom, and compassion. The Tibetan Book of the Dead provides detailed guidance and practices for traversing these intermediate states skillfully. These include meditation practices, prayers, and visualization techniques aimed at recognizing the nature of mind, overcoming fear and attachment, and directing consciousness towards a favorable rebirth or enlightenment.

The teachings emphasize the importance of maintaining awareness, compassion, and a clear understanding of the Dharma during the Bardo stages. By doing so, practitioners can transform their experiences in the Bardo into opportunities for spiritual growth and ultimately, liberation.

The concept of the Bardo and its teachings are not solely relevant to the deceased or dying. They hold invaluable insights and lessons for the living, offering a roadmap to navigate the challenges and uncertainties of life. Understanding the Bardo teaches us to live mindfully, to face our fears and attachments, and to cultivate compassion and wisdom.

Navigating the Principal Bardos

Navigating through the "Bardo Thödol," we encounter a structured approach that divides the text into three distinct main sections: the Chikhai Bardo, the Chonyid Bardo, and the Sidpa Bardo. Each serves a specific purpose and addresses different aspects of the death-rebirth continuum, acting as guideposts to help the reader and practitioner orient themselves in the rich and complex landscape of Tibetan Buddhist thought on life, death, and what lies beyond. This structured division is essential, as it organizes the profound teachings and insights of the text into manageable and comprehensible segments, facilitating a deeper understanding and appreciation of the wisdom encapsulated within.

Each of these sections is a piece of a larger puzzle, contributing to the holistic understanding of the transitionary states and offering guidance and clarity for both the deceased and the living. As we delve into each of these bardos, we will explore their unique characteristics, teachings, and the significance they hold within the overarching narrative of the "Bardo Thödol." Through this exploration, we aim to unravel the threads of wisdom woven into the text and bring forth the depth and richness that have made it a timeless guide for those seeking to understand the mysteries of existence and transcendence.

One of the foundational elements of the "Bardo Thödol" is the extensive meditation and visualization practices it prescribes. These are not arbitrary; they are integral to preparing the mind for the experiences of the bardos. The meditations are multifaceted, focusing on aspects such as cultivating mindfulness, developing compassion, and recognizing the nature of the mind. Visualization practices often accompany these meditations, where practitioners visualize deities, lights, and symbols, each representing different aspects of enlightened mind, aiding in transforming ordinary perception to enlightened wisdom.

The text also lays out a series of rituals and prayers, each serving a specific purpose in aiding the deceased through the bardos. The rituals are not just ceremonial; they are imbued with symbolic meaning, each action, each recitation is a step towards guiding the consciousness towards a favorable rebirth. The prayers are often recited by the lamas and the loved ones, sending waves of positive energy and blessings, assisting the deceased in their journey.

Moral and ethical teachings are woven into the fabric of the "Bardo Thödol." These teachings serve as a compass, guiding the practitioner in living a life aligned with the principles of compassion, generosity, and right conduct. The text elucidates the law of karma, the cause and effect of actions, and how living ethically creates the foundation for a favorable future, both in life and after death.

The "Bardo Thödol" is rich in psychological insights. It delves into the workings of the mind, exploring the nature of consciousness, the dynamics of emotions, and the play of thoughts. The text provides a detailed description of how the mind experiences, perceives, and reacts during the different bardos, offering guidance on recognizing illusions and awakening to the true nature of reality.

Philosophically, the text is a profound exploration of Tibetan Buddhist doctrines. It discusses the nature of existence, the concept of emptiness, the illusion of duality, and the potential for enlightenment. The "Bardo Thödol" invites us to question, to contemplate, and to realize the deeper truths of existence, encouraging a shift from ignorance to wisdom, from suffering to liberation.

In essence, the "Bardo Thödol" is a comprehensive guide, encompassing a vast array of teachings and practices, each aimed at illuminating the path towards liberation. It invites us to engage deeply, to reflect, to practice, and ultimately, to awaken to our innate wisdom and compassion.

Chapter One

Chikhai Bardo: The Bardo of Dying

Introduction

As we gently tread into the realm of the Tibetan Book of the Dead we find ourselves at the gateway of the Chikhai Bardo, aptly named The Bardo of the Moment of Death. This initial bardo is the genesis of the spiritual odyssey, a juncture where the journey of consciousness begins, stepping into realms untethered by the physical body.

The Chikhai Bardo holds a distinctive place within the "Bardo Thödol," serving as the foundation upon which the entire spiritual journey is constructed. It sets the stage for the ensuing bardos, establishing the initial conditions and experiences that influence the trajectory of the consciousness through the subsequent transitional states. It is here that the seeds of realization or delusion are sown, determining the course of the journey through the bardo realms and beyond.

This bardo functions as a mirror reflecting the culmination of a lifetime's practice and understanding, offering the first opportunities for recognition and liberation. The experiences and realizations encountered here resonate through the tapestry of the text, influencing the unfolding narrative and the potential for awakening in the later stages.

The exploration of the Chikhai Bardo provides a foundation for understanding the interconnectedness and continuity of the teachings within the "Bardo Thö-dol." It invites us to perceive the text not as a collection of isolated teachings, but as an integrated whole, where each bardo, each teaching, each practice is a thread woven into the intricate fabric of the journey towards enlightenment.

Dissolution of the Elements and the Physical Body

As we start exploring the Chikhai Bardo, we approach the inevitable—death itself. Here, we witness a transformative event, a kind of cosmic dance—the dissolution of elements and the physical body. This dance, characterized by the unraveling of our elemental composition, acts as a gateway from the tangible world we know to the mysteries that lie beyond.

Imagine, if you will, our being as a harmonious composition of five fundamental elements: earth, water, fire, air, and space. These aren't just scientific terms; they represent the essence, the vitality that breathes life into our physical form. The journey through the Chikhai Bardo is a return to this elemental purity, a shedding of the corporeal to embrace the ethereal.

The first curtain falls with the earth element dissolving into water. It's like feeling the ground beneath you become a mere whisper, the solidity and structure of the body fading, leaving behind a sense of merging with the world around, a blurring of the boundaries that once defined us.

Following this, the water element, our internal fluidity and cohesion, begins to merge with fire. Imagine the rivers within us drying up, the sensation of life's essence slowly withdrawing, like the gentle receding of tides leaving the shore barren.

Next, we experience the fire element, our inner warmth and transformative energy, integrating into air. It's a sunset within the self, a gradual cooling, a dimming of the internal flame that once danced vibrantly.

Finally, the air element, the breath of life, whispers into the vastness of space. It's a moment of profound stillness and silence, a pause in the rhythm of existence, as the breath becomes one with the cosmos.

This culminating silence isn't the end; it's a prologue to the revelation of the Clear Light, the inherent luminosity of the mind, pure, unobstructed, and serene. This is not a light you see with the eyes; it's an inner awakening, a recognition of the divine spark within.

What we are exploring here, in this stage of the "Bardo Thödol," is more than a philosophical concept. It's a lived experience, a deeply personal journey through the threshold of death. This dissolution is not just about the end; it's a reflection on the transitory nature of life, a meditation on the dance between existence and non-existence.

As we navigate through this sacred terrain, we're not just observers; we're active participants in unraveling the mysteries of life, death, and what lies beyond. The teachings of the Chikhai Bardo are a lantern in the dark, a guide helping us to cultivate understanding, compassion, and a realization of the deeper truths woven into the fabric of our existence.

The Clear Light of Reality

Venturing deeper into the Chikhai Bardo, we find ourselves at a pivotal moment of unparalleled significance—the encounter with the Clear Light of Reality. This isn't a fleeting glimpse but a precious gateway, a culmination of lifetimes of seeking, where the inherent unity of existence is revealed.

Representing the essence of ultimate reality, the Clear Light is a luminous truth awaiting recognition. For the adept practitioner, versed in mindfulness and refined by meditation, this moment transforms into a sacred communion, an intimate merging with the radiant essence. Here, individual awareness dissolves into the boundless, illuminating the path to liberation and bringing enlightenment within reach.

However, for the unprepared, the brilliance of the Clear Light might remain concealed, highlighting the indispensability of the teachings of the "Bardo Thödol". In this sacred juncture, layers of ignorance, or avidya, act as veils shrouding our true nature, much like mist hiding the valleys and peaks of a mountainous terrain. Our vision becomes distorted; we see shadows and shapes, yet miss the luminous essence of reality.

Along the journey, we also encounter shadows of our past—our karmic obscurations. These shadows are imprints of our actions, footprints in the snow shaping the landscapes of our minds, weaving our experiences, and often obscuring the brilliance of the Clear Light.

Emotional and mental afflictions accompany us, acting like persistent clouds shadowing our path with attachment, aversion, and delusion, preventing the radiant dawn of recognition. Additionally, our attachment to the self, a sense of 'I' that feels real and solid, fosters a dualistic perception that veils the non-dual nature of the Clear Light.

Navigating the terrains of the Bardo, we may face unwelcome travelers of fear and disorientation, which stir the waters of our minds, obscuring the serene reflection needed for recognizing the Clear Light. Familiarity with the path is indispensable; without prior experience and reflection on the essence of the Clear Light, recognition in the Bardo becomes akin to finding a needle in a cosmic haystack.

The "Bardo Thödol" prescribes practices and teachings aimed at peeling away these veils, refining our perception, and revealing the luminous nature inherent in all beings. By integrating mindfulness, compassion, and wisdom into daily life, practitioners prepare to meet this unique juncture with awareness and understanding, recognizing the Clear Light as their true nature.

This unveiling is more than an ephemeral experience; it's a golden opportunity for immediate liberation, an invitation to awaken to our innate wisdom and compassion, to reflect on life's impermanence, and to live with mindfulness and spiritual vigor. The teachings of this Bardo serve as a guide for the dying and a reflective mirror for the living, unveiling deeper truths of existence and offering a path towards self-realization and liberation.

Embarking on the journey through the "Bardo Thödol" is not merely an intellectual endeavor; it's a profound spiritual odyssey. It prompts us to reflect deeply on life's impermanence and the interconnected tapestry of existence, beckoning us to live with purpose, cultivate devotion, and nurture the qualities essential for embracing the Clear Light of Reality when the moment arrives.

Meditation and Visualization Practice

Delving into the heart of the Chikhai Bardo we uncover a treasure trove of meditation and visualization practices designed to illuminate the path to and lift the various illusionary veils.

Meditation in the Chikhai Bardo is an invitation to inner stillness, a call to plunge into the depths of consciousness and embrace the pulsating silence that resides there. The text elucidates various meditation techniques, each tailored to guide practitioners through the dissolution of elements, enabling them to witness the dance of life and death with equanimity and insight.

Visualization practices within this Bardo are presented as vibrant tapestries woven from the threads of sacred imagery and divine archetypes. The "Bardo Thödol" offers a kaleidoscope of visualizations, each infused with symbolic meaning, guiding the practitioner to invoke and embody divine energies.

The union of meditation and visualization in the Chikhai Bardo forms a symphony of transformative practices. The "Bardo Thödol" meticulously details how these practices intertwine, creating a harmonious dance that guides the practitioner through the veils of reality to the threshold of liberation. The text serves as a compassionate guide, holding the practitioner's hand, illuminating the path, and whispering the ancient melodies of wisdom and truth.

Embarking on the practices within the Chikhai Bardo is akin to sailing on a sacred river whose waters are infused with the essence of enlightenment. The "Bardo Thödol" is the navigator, the practices are the vessel, and the destination is the luminous shore of the Clear Light of Reality.

Here is a selection of practices:

Recognition of the Clear Light:

Objective: To enable practitioners to recognize and merge with the intrinsic luminosity of the mind at the moment of death.

Technique: Practitioners cultivate familiarity with this luminosity through deep meditation, often guided by a master, focusing on the nature of mind and attempting to maintain awareness during transitions such as falling asleep and waking up. This practice aims to simulate the process of dying, fostering recognition of the Clear Light when it manifests.

Visualizing the Dissolution of Elements:

Objective: To mentally rehearse the dissolution process of the elements (earth into water, water into fire, fire into air, and air into space) that occurs during death.

Technique: Practitioners visualize each element dissolving into the next, culminating in the experience of the 'clear light of death.' This meditation enhances awareness and understanding of the transition from the physical body to a subtler form of existence.

Practices of Phowa:

Objective: To transfer consciousness at the time of death to a pure land or a higher state of being.

Technique: Practitioners concentrate on visualizing channels and energies within the body, and through controlled breathing and intention, they practice the 'ejection of consciousness,' simulating its transfer to a Buddhafield.

Deity Yoga and Guru Yoga:

Objective: To invoke the enlightened energies of deities or the guru, fostering a connection that aids recognition of the Clear Light.

Technique: Through detailed visualization, mantra recitation, and devotion, practitioners seek to embody the qualities of the chosen deity or guru, creating a conducive mental state for liberation.

Heart-Centered Meditation:

Objective: To cultivate love, compassion, and openness, essential qualities for facing the unknown realms of the Bardo with grace.

Technique: Practitioners focus on the heart center, generating feelings of love and compassion, radiating these qualities outward to all beings, and contemplating the interdependence of all life.

These practices serve as a spiritual compass, guiding practitioners through the Chikhai Bardo with heightened awareness and presence. By engaging earnestly in these techniques, one cultivates the wisdom and insight necessary to navigate the luminosities and shadows of this sacred terrain, seizing the unique opportunity for awakening and liberation.

Philosophical Doctrines

As we gracefully transition from the meditation and visualization practices that unravel the sublime Clear Light of Reality, it is time to gently steer our minds toward the profound philosophical doctrines embedded within the Chikhai Bardo. Here, the melodies of truth that have been softly playing in the background are brought to the fore, revealing deeper, more intricate harmonies and insights.

One of the first doctrines we encounter illuminates the intrinsic purity and luminosity of the mind, often referred to as "Rigpa" in Tibetan Buddhism. This state, akin to the vastness of the clear sky unmarred by passing clouds, is the inherent nature of the mind. Recognizing and resting in this nature is key to liberation. We are guided through practices such as sky-gazing, where we allow our minds to merge with the vast openness, experiencing the unobstructed nature of Rigpa, and witnessing the transient nature of phenomena without attachment or aversion.

We then delve into the transient nature of life, as vividly portrayed in the Chikhai Bardo. Here, we learn that embracing impermanence opens the heart to the infinite possibilities of each moment and fosters a deep appreciation for the preciousness of human life. Visualizing an ever-flowing river, we internalize the fluidity and transient nature of existence, fostering a deeper acceptance of change and loss.

In the harmonious dance of interdependence and emptiness, we discern the subtle connections that bind all phenomena and uncover the profound truth of inherent non-existence. These doctrines serve as our compass, navigating us through the multifaceted landscapes of the Bardo and guiding our steps on the path to liberation. We reflect upon the intricate web of interdependence that connects all beings, fostering a sense of universal responsibility and compassion, and urging us to cultivate love and altruism.

The intricate mosaic of karma weaves the stories of our actions, words, and thoughts, revealing the manifold realms of possibilities that lie ahead. The teachings on rebirth unveil the cyclical nature of existence, inviting us to ponder the transient and interconnected fabric of life and death. Meditating upon a tree, nourished by the earth, water, air, and sun, we realize our interconnectedness and cultivate gratitude and compassion for all.

At the heart of the Chikhai Bardo's philosophical wisdom is the teaching of liberation through recognition. The doctrines delve deeper into this realization, shedding light on how embracing our inherent nature can free us from the cycles of existence. The teachings resonate as a call to awaken to our intrinsic purity and to see through the illusions that veil our true selves. Meditating on a rainbow, practitioners explore the transient and ungraspable beauty of phenomena, inviting a non-dualistic perception of reality.

The resonance of compassion and the cultivation of Bodhicitta play a significant role in guiding our journey. The melody of altruistic love and intention for enlightenment is enriched and emphasized, leading us through shadows and into the warm embrace of enlightenment.

As we immerse ourselves in the philosophical treasures of the Chikhai Bardo, we find the teachings are not merely echoes of what we have learned but are revelations of deeper wisdom and insights. The doctrines herein invite us to reflect more intimately on the self and the cosmos, nurturing our awareness, compassion, and yearning for truth, as we prepare to fully embrace the Clear Light of Reality and the boundless enlightenment it promises.

In this sacred exploration, the Chikhai Bardo becomes more than a passage in the "Bardo Thödol"; it is a spiritual symphony, each note resonating with timeless wisdom and each doctrine a pathway to enlightenment. The teachings and practices unveiled in this Bardo are not just for those at the threshold of death; they are reflective mirrors for all of us, offering glimpses into the deeper truths of existence and guiding us on our continual journey towards self-realization and liberation.

Psychological Insights

Delving even deeper, we embark on a journey into the realm of psychological insights, where ancient wisdom intertwines with the intricacies of the human mind. The Chikhai Bardo, with its vivid and allegorical teachings, unfolds a panorama of inner landscapes, beckoning us to explore the uncharted territories of our consciousness.

Within this Bardo, we uncover the labyrinth of our psyche, examining the multifarious layers of our thoughts, emotions, and perceptions. The teachings guide us in unravelling the threads of our mental patterns, exposing the underlying dynamics that shape our experience of reality.

One of the most compelling psychological insights gleaned from the Chikhai Bardo is the concept of the shadow self. In the luminous expanse of the mind, the shadow represents the unacknowledged and repressed aspects of our being. The teachings invite us to face these shadows, to embrace them with compassion and understanding, allowing for transformation and healing.

As we navigate through the shadows, we encounter the archetypal figures and symbolic imagery that populate the landscape of the Bardo. These archetypes, manifestations of our deepest fears and desires, serve as mirrors reflecting the complexities of our inner world. Engaging with them, we unearth the latent potentials and hidden strengths that reside within the recesses of our psyche.

The Chikhai Bardo also reveals the interplay between duality and unity, offering insights into the dualistic nature of the mind and the unity of existence. Here, we contemplate the paradox of separateness and oneness, discovering the interconnectedness that permeates all of life. This realization invites us to transcend the limitations of the egoic mind, awakening to the boundless nature of our true selves.

In this exploration of psychological insights, mindfulness and contemplation are our steadfast companions. The teachings encourage us to cultivate a mindful presence, observing the ebb and flow of our thoughts and emotions without attachment or aversion. Through contemplation, we delve into the depths of our being, uncovering the pearls of wisdom that lie beneath the surface of our conscious awareness.

The teachings of the Chikhai Bardo illuminate the path to self-realization, fostering a deeper understanding of our inner world and guiding us towards psychological and spiritual integration. The wisdom embedded within this Bardo invites us to reflect upon our mental constructs, to discern the transient from the eternal, and to embrace the journey towards wholeness.

As we immerse ourselves in the psychological insights within the Chikhai Bardo, we encounter the transformative power of self-awareness. The journey, while filled with challenges and revelations, is ultimately one of liberation. The teachings beckon us to shed the layers of illusion, to awaken to our inherent purity, and to step into the light of self-realization.

With every step, we are reminded of the impermanence of life, the interconnectedness of all beings, and the potential that resides within us. The Chikhai Bardo, a guide through the landscapes of the mind, becomes a beacon of light, illuminating the path towards enlightenment and liberation.

Chapter Two

Chonyid Bardo: The Bardo of Dharmata

Introduction

Stepping beyond the threshold of the Chikhai Bardo, we find ourselves delving into the depths of the Chonyid Bardo, aptly titled The Bardo of the Experiencing of Reality. The atmosphere of this Bardo is rich with vivid imagery, kaleidoscopic colors, and a symphony of sounds, representing the diverse manifestations of both enlightened and unenlightened states of being.

To venture into the realm of the Chonyid Bardo is to embrace a world where every beat and rhythm is meaningful. This realm is a mirror, reflecting not just the vastness of the cosmos but the intricate landscapes of our inner selves. The dances we encounter here are deeply significant, for they carry the potential of liberation, of enlightenment, and of a profound understanding of the nature of existence.

The transition from the Chikhai Bardo to the Chonyid Bardo is akin to emerging from a dreamless slumber into a vivid tapestry of dreams. In the Chikhai Bardo, we glimpsed the pristine and luminous nature of the mind, a clear light consciousness, unadorned and unfettered. But as we step into the Chonyid Bardo, this clarity morphs into myriad forms, and the dance of visions begins.

This transition is delicate, a subtle shift of consciousness, where the tranquil clear light gives birth to vibrant and dynamic visions. It's a moment of awakening, not to the physical world we left behind, but to a realm teeming with possibilities, challenges, and profound teachings.

As we wade deeper into the Chonyid Bardo, a cascade of experiences unfolds. The realm is alive with both serene and wrathful deities, symbolic manifestations of our intrinsic qualities and obstacles. These deities are not external entities but reflections of our own mind, inviting us to dance, to understand, and to transcend.

The visions in the Chonyid Bardo are as varied as they are profound. They range from the tranquil and benevolent to the fierce and daunting, each a symbolic representation of aspects of enlightenment and impediments to it. The dance floor is illuminated by divine lights and resonates with celestial sounds, guiding, warning, and teaching.

Here, in this vibrant realm, every vision is a teacher and every experience a lesson. It's a dance of self and cosmos, a choreography of becoming and un-becoming. Each step we take, each vision we encounter, is an opportunity to understand the nature of existence and to move closer to liberation.

As we traverse this bardo, let us open our hearts to the teachings it holds. Let us dance with the visions, learn the rhythms of the cosmos, and move gracefully towards understanding and enlightenment. The Chonyid Bardo invites us to a dance of realization, where every step is a journey inward, and every beat a heartbeat of the cosmos.

The Dawning of Peaceful Deities

As we delve deeper into the vibrant realm of the Chonyid Bardo, the first to grace the cosmic dance floor are the peaceful deities. These deities, emanating serenity and wisdom, are not external beings but reflections of our innermost nature, aspects of our enlightened mind. In their presence, the Chonyid Bardo becomes a sacred ground where the dance of self-discovery and transformation unfolds.

The peaceful deities are embodiments of compassion, wisdom, and the myriad positive qualities of our consciousness. Each deity carries a unique symbolism, representing different facets of the enlightened mind. They appear in various forms, radiating colors that mirror the richness of our inner world, holding objects that symbolize the tools we have within us for liberation. In their serene gaze, we find reflections of our potential for boundless love, profound insight, and unwavering equanimity.

The symbolism of these deities is rich and multilayered, inviting us to explore the depths of our being. They signify the inherent purity and goodness of our nature, and their presence is a reminder of our potential for enlightenment. Each deity, with its unique attributes, invites us to recognize the divine qualities within us, to embrace our innate wisdom, and to dance to the rhythm of compassion and love.

Interacting with these peaceful deities is a profound experience, a sacred dialogue between the finite and the infinite. It's an invitation to look within, to recognize the divine in the mundane, the extraordinary in the ordinary. As we engage with them, we are not merely observers but active participants in this divine dance. We learn to see beyond the veil of illusion, to recognize the deities as aspects of our true nature, and to embrace the teachings they impart.

The teachings of the peaceful deities revolve around recognition and liberation. They guide us to see beyond the surface, to recognize our innate purity and divinity. They teach us that liberation is not a distant goal but a present possibility, available in every moment, in every breath. Through their wisdom, we learn to let go of our clinging and aversions, to dance freely in the present moment, and to move gracefully towards the state of enlightenment.

The Emergence of Wrathful Deities

In the intricate dance of the Chonyid Bardo, following the serene waltz of the peaceful deities, there emerges a vigorous, tempestuous rhythm, heralding the arrival of the wrathful deities. The atmosphere shifts; the celestial dance floor vibrates with intensity as these formidable figures make their presence known. Their appearance, imbued with symbolism and potency, might at first evoke trepidation, but their emergence is as vital as the dawn of their peaceful counterparts.

The wrathful deities are awe-inspiring, their forms resplendent with powerful symbolism. They may appear fierce, with glaring eyes and gnashing teeth, surrounded by flames, depicting the transformative fire of wisdom. However, beneath their ferocious exterior lies a profound wisdom and compassion. Their wrath is not directed at us but rather at our ignorance, our attachments, and the illusions that bind us to suffering. They are the embodiment of enlightened energy, the fierce aspect of compassion that cuts through delusion and liberates us from the shackles of our own making.

Understanding the nature and purpose of the wrathful deities is a journey into the heart of our fears and illusions. They are mirrors reflecting our inner demons, our unresolved conflicts, and the shadows we often shy away from. Their ferocity is a call to face these aspects of ourselves, to confront and reconcile with the parts we'd rather ignore. The wrathful deities invite us to dance with our fears, to embrace the transformative power of their energy, and to emerge from this dance with a deeper understanding and a liberated heart.

Facing the wrathful deities requires strategies for recognition and reconciliation. We are called to look beyond their formidable appearance and recognize them as manifestations of our own enlightened nature. This recognition is not an intellectual understanding but a heartfelt realization, a direct experience of our intrinsic purity and wisdom. Reconciliation with the wrathful deities involves embracing our shadows, integrating our fears, and transforming the energy of our conflicts into the light of wisdom. It is a dance of transformation, where the fierce energy of the deities becomes the fuel for our enlightenment.

The pathway to liberation through fear is a profound aspect of the emergence of the wrathful deities. Fear, often seen as an obstacle, becomes the gateway to liberation. The intensity of the wrathful deities evokes our deepest fears, bringing them to the surface, making them visible and tangible. Facing these fears, dancing with them, and transforming them into wisdom is the essence of the path of liberation. The wrathful deities guide us through this dance, their fierce compassion illuminating the shadows and leading us to the light of realization.

Navigating the Luminous Visions

Amidst the dance with both peaceful and wrathful deities in the Chonyid Bardo, the spiritual traveler encounters a canvas of luminous visions, each a brushstroke painting the depth and complexity of the human psyche and spiritual potential. These visions, resplendent in their diversity, are not mere illusions, but revelations and reflections, guiding lights on the path to liberation.

The nature of these visions is as manifold as it is profound. They can be vivid and overwhelming, subtle and intricate, each imbued with symbols and imagery that hold the keys to unraveling the depth of our being. Like cosmic riddles, they beckon the traveler to look deeper, to question and explore, to uncover the layers of meaning and significance hidden within their radiant folds.

Interpreting the symbols and imagery of the visions is a delicate dance of insight and intuition. It requires a heart open to mystery and a mind sharp with discernment. Each symbol, each image, is a piece of a celestial puzzle, revealing aspects of our inner world, our aspirations, fears, desires, and the boundless potential for enlightenment that resides within us. The visions invite us to reflect, to contemplate, to engage with the wisdom they hold, and to integrate this wisdom into the fabric of our being.

Our personal karma plays a pivotal role in shaping and influencing the visions we encounter. Like a skilled artist, it crafts the scenes, the characters, the narratives that unfold before our spiritual eyes. Our past actions, thoughts, and intentions, the seeds of karma we have sown, bloom into the visions that guide our journey through the Chonyid Bardo. They are reflections of our spiritual history, mirrors showing us the paths we have walked and the landscapes we have shaped through our choices and actions.

Utilizing the visions for liberation is the essence of navigating the luminous landscapes of the Chonyid Bardo. The visions are not mere spectacles to be observed but sacred texts to be read, understood, and lived. They are teachings, guideposts, invitations to transform and transcend, to rise above our limitations and step into the boundless freedom of our true nature. By engaging with the visions, by embracing the wisdom they impart, and by integrating this wisdom into our being, we walk the path of liberation, moving ever closer to the realization of our divine potential.

The Sounds, Lights, and Rays

In the transformative landscape of the Chonyid Bardo, the spiritual wanderer is not only greeted by visions, but also enveloped by the resounding harmonies of divine sounds, the enchanting display of celestial lights, and the guiding brilliance of spiritual rays.

The phenomena of divine sounds and lights are as varied as they are profound. The sounds range from ethereal melodies to powerful resonances, each note a vibration of cosmic wisdom. The lights, radiant and diverse, shimmer in hues that speak the language of the divine, painting the canvas of the spiritual sky with messages of truth and illumination. These are not ordinary sounds and lights, but expressions of the divine, manifestations of the ultimate reality, resonating and shining forth the essence of enlightenment.

The significance of these divine sounds and lights lies in their ability to communicate, to convey teachings and truths beyond the grasp of words. They speak to the heart, to the innermost being, bypassing the limitations of the conceptual mind. Interpreting these divine expressions requires a tuning of the spiritual ear and eye, a receptivity to the subtle messages and insights they impart. They are guides, teachers, illuminating the path and resonating the truths that lead to liberation.

Aligning with the rays for liberation is akin to tuning a musical instrument to the harmonies of the cosmos. These rays, streams of divine light and wisdom, are pathways leading to the source, guiding lines drawn on the canvas of the spiritual journey. Aligning with them involves attunement, a harmonizing of one's being with the vibrations and frequencies of divine truth. It is a dance of unity, a merging with the cosmic rhythm, a step into the flow of divine grace.

The interaction between sounds, lights, and consciousness is a symphony of spiritual awakening. The sounds and lights are not external phenomena but reflections of our inner being, resonances of our divine nature. Our consciousness, the listener and observer, engages with these divine expressions, dances with the melodies and hues, and in this dance, is transformed. The sounds and lights awaken the dormant potentials within, ignite the flames of wisdom, and illuminate the shadows of ignorance, guiding consciousness towards the realization of its true nature.

Psychological and Spiritual Transformation

In the unfolding journey of the Chonyid Bardo, the soul embarks on a profound psychological and spiritual metamorphosis. It is here, amidst the celestial lights and divine resonances, that the heart undergoes a crucible of transformation, delving deep into the inner sanctum of the self. The Chonyid Bardo, with its myriad of experiences, serves as a canvas upon which the inner work of the soul is intricately painted, shaping the contours of the spiritual journey.

The inner work in Chonyid Bardo is as multifaceted as it is transformative. The soul, acting as both the artisan and the canvas, confronts the depth of its being, facing the shadows and illuminating the light within. The work is internal, but its reverberations are cosmic, resonating the echoes of self-realization and divine communion. It is a dance of self and spirit, an intimate embrace of the human and the divine.

Facing and transforming fears and desires are pivotal elements of this inner journey. Fears, those shadows that cloud the light of the soul, are met with the illuminating gaze of awareness. They are not enemies to be defeated, but companions to be understood, aspects of the self seeking recognition and transformation. Desires, the flames that fuel the journey, are tempered by the waters of wisdom, reshaped into aspirations that align with the higher purpose. The dance with fears and desires is a dance of fire and light, a transformative alchemy that shapes the spiritual gold of the soul.

The process of ego dissolution is a cornerstone of this transformative journey. The ego, the constructed self, the mask of identity, begins to unravel, revealing the true face of the divine within. It is a shedding of illusions, a peeling away of layers, unveiling the essence of being. The ego is not annihilated, but transformed, reshaped into a transparent vessel for the divine light. The dissolution is a rebirth, a phoenix rising from the ashes of the false self, soaring into the boundless skies of true nature.

Embracing change and impermanence is the rhythm of this dance. The soul learns the art of letting go, the grace of surrender, the beauty of transience. Every moment is a brushstroke on the canvas of existence, every experience a note in the symphony of life. Impermanence is not a foe, but a friend, a teacher of the eternal dance of creation and dissolution. In the embrace of change, the soul finds the stillness within the movement, the permanence within the transience, the divine within the human.

Practices and Prayers for Liberation

Navigating the waters of the Chonyid Bardo demands a compass of essential practices, rituals steeped in ancient wisdom and celestial grace. These practices are the anchors amidst the ephemeral waves, the lighthouses illuminating the path to liberation. They are the harmonious melodies that guide the soul, the sacred rhythms that attune the heart to the divine symphony of the cosmos. Visualization and meditation techniques form the bedrock of these essential practices. The mind, a potent artist, crafts luminous images, divine tableaus that guide the soul through the celestial landscapes. Meditation, the sacred dance of stillness, invites the traveler into the heart of presence, the sanctuary of the now, where the divine whispers are heard, and the light of wisdom is seen.

Prayer and devotion play a pivotal role in this spiritual tapestry. They are the golden threads weaving through the canvas, connecting the soul to the divine, the finite to the infinite. Prayer is the sacred dialogue, the intimate conversation between the heart and the cosmos, the whisper of the soul echoing through the celestial spheres. Devotion is the divine dance, the rhythmic movement of the heart attuned to the cosmic melody, the embrace of the lover and the beloved. Through prayer and devotion, the soul is enveloped in celestial grace, guided by divine love, and illuminated by the light of spiritual wisdom.

Compassion and altruism are the sacred wings upon which the soul soars through the realms of the Chonyid Bardo. They are the divine winds that uplift the heart, the celestial currents that guide the traveler towards the shores of liberation. Compassion is the heartbeat of the cosmos, the rhythmic pulse of divine love that flows through all of existence. Altruism is the sacred breath, the divine exhale that breathes life into the world, the celestial whisper that echoes the call of love. Through compassion and altruism, the soul becomes a vessel of divine love, a beacon of celestial light, and a channel of cosmic grace.

These practices and prayers, these sacred tools and divine whispers, guide the traveler through the luminous realms of the Chonyid Bardo. They are the brushstrokes on the canvas of liberation, the hues of divine love painting the masterpiece of spiritual freedom. Through essential practices, through prayer and devotion, through visualization and meditation, through compassion and altruism, the soul navigates the waters of the intermediary state, guided by the lighthouse of divine wisdom, and embraced by the arms of celestial love.

Chapter Three

Sidpa Bardo: The Bardo of Becoming

Introduction

Venturing into the Sidpa Bardo, also called the Bardo of Becoming, we are greeted by interwoven destinies and uncharted potentials. This Bardo of Rebirth bridges the transient nature of life and the enduring essence of the soul. Within its bounds, souls are guided by the teachings and wisdom accumulated thus far, delving into a journey marked by self-discovery and transformation.

The Sidpa Bardo is not a mere passage but a realm rich with lessons and revelations, where the ephemeral nature of life meets the timeless truths of existence. Here, the soul is presented with the opportunity to reflect on past experiences and the essence of its being, shedding light on the karmic imprints and spiritual learnings that shape the journey ahead.

This bardo also lays bare the foundational Buddhist principles of impermanence and interconnectedness. The soul bears witness to the ever-changing nature of existence, recognizing the transient yet interconnected web of life. This understanding fosters a deeper appreciation for the preciousness of human life and the boundless opportunities for spiritual growth it presents.

Guided by the light of awareness and armed with the teachings of the Dharma, the soul traverses the landscapes of the Sidpa Bardo, seeking alignment with its higher purpose and the liberation from the cyclical nature of Samsara. The choices made within this realm are influenced by the clarity of understanding and the depth of compassion cultivated, shaping the conditions for the impending rebirth.

The Interplay of Karma and Rebirth

The Role of Karma in Rebirth is akin to a skilled artisan sculpting the clay of existence. It is the unseen hand that shapes our journey, carving out paths of enlightenment and shadow in equal measure. Karma, in its infinite wisdom, is not a mere system of cause and effect, but a sacred dance of actions and reactions, shaping the rhythm of our rebirth. Every thought, every deed, every whisper of the heart leaves its imprint, guiding the soul towards its next incarnation, painting the canvas of our next life with the hues of our actions.

Accumulated Wisdom and Teachings are the guiding stars in the vast expanse of the Sidpa Bardo. The wisdom garnered through lifetimes acts as a beacon of light, illuminating the path towards liberation. This wisdom is not a mere accumulation of teachings but the very essence of our spiritual journey, a harmonious melody composed of experiences, learnings, and realizations. It is the golden thread that weaves through the fabric of our existence, connecting us to the divine teachings of Buddha and the eternal truths of the universe.

Trials arise like mountains on the horizon, each peak representing a karmic debt to be acknowledged and reconciled. The wanderer faces reflections of unfulfilled promises, unkindness, and missed opportunities for compassion. Yet, within the crevices of these trials, wisdom and forgiveness bloom, guiding lights on the path to renewal.

The Interplay of Karma and Dharma is a celestial dance, a symphony of cosmic energies harmonizing to create the melody of existence. Dharma, the eternal law of the cosmos, guides the dance of karma, shaping its rhythm, its tempo, its every move. It is in this sacred dance that we find the balance between action and reaction, between the seen and the unseen, between the ephemeral and the eternal. The dance of Karma and Dharma is the heartbeat of the universe, the pulsating rhythm that guides our journey through the Sidpa Bardo towards rebirth and beyond.

Navigating Choices and Destiny

Within the labyrinth of the Sidpa Bardo, souls find themselves at a crossroads, caught in a celestial dance between free will and determinism, each step a brushstroke painting their destiny. Navigating Choices and Destiny in this bardo is akin to a leaf gracefully navigating the currents of a mighty river, with the undercurrents of past lives and the gentle breezes of compassion and wisdom shaping its journey.

The Dance Between Free Will and Determinism is a harmonious yet intricate ballet, where every pirouette and plié is imbued with cosmic significance. Here, free will is not merely the ability to choose but is the divine spark that ignites the flame of self-awareness, illuminating the path of liberation. Determinism, on the other hand, is the cosmic rhythm, the divine melody that orchestrates the symphony of existence. Navigating this dance is to embrace the fluidity of existence, to find the balance between the ebb and flow of the cosmic tide and the whispering winds of the soul's desires.

Within the Sidpa Bardo, a labyrinth of choices unfurls before the soul. Every turn, every crossroad is laden with the potential for enlightenment or further entanglement in the web of samsara. The dance between free will and determinism reaches a crescendo here, as the traveler's decisions carve the path towards rebirth.

The Impact of Past Lives echoes through the corridors of the Sidpa Bardo like a timeless melody, a symphony composed of actions and reactions, of love and loss, of joy and sorrow. Each past life is a note in this melody, a harmonic vibration that shapes the soul's journey. The echoes of past lives are not mere remnants of a bygone era but are the building blocks of the soul's identity, the foundation upon which the edifice of spiritual evolution is built.

Moral and Ethical Teachings

Navigating the swirling currents of existence, the moral and ethical teachings emerge as guiding lights through the fog of uncertainty. These teachings aren't rigid commandments, but fluid melodies that resonate deeply within us, encouraging us to align with the universal principles of love, compassion, and wisdom.

The teachings emphasize the importance of right intention, right speech, and right action, encouraging us to cultivate a heart that beats in unison with the rhythm of the cosmos. They remind us of the ripple effect of our thoughts, words, and deeds, urging us to be mindful of the energy we send out into the world, for it will inevitably circle back to us, either as a gentle breeze or a stormy gust.

One of the core tenets of these teachings is the cultivation of compassion—an all-encompassing love that sees beyond the illusion of separateness and recognizes the inherent interconnectedness of all beings. It's about embracing the other as an extension of the self, understanding that their joy and suffering are intrinsically linked to our own. It is this cultivation of compassion that acts as a key, unlocking the doors to a higher realm of existence, where altruism becomes the natural way of being.

Furthermore, the teachings encourage us to tread the path of ethical living, to be conscientious in our actions, and to uphold the values of truth, integrity, and kindness. It's about making conscious choices that are in harmony with the greater good, about living in a way that is sustainable and beneficial for all sentient beings and the planet.

Delving deeper, we uncover the wisdom of balance, of walking the middle way, avoiding the extremes of self-indulgence and self-denial. It's about finding equilibrium, harmonizing the inner and outer, the material and the spiritual, understanding that true fulfillment arises not from the accumulation of external possessions but from the richness of the inner landscape.

Rituals and Prayers for Navigating Rebirth

Within the mystical aspects of the Sidpa Bardo, the delicate threads of rituals and prayers weave a path of luminous light, guiding the wandering consciousness towards the sacred dance of rebirth. These ancient practices, imbued with the wisdom of the sages, serve as a celestial compass, aligning our inner world with the cosmic rhythms and leading us towards liberation.

The rituals in the Sidpa Bardo are not mere ceremonial acts; they are the sacred symphony of the universe, resonating with the divine frequencies that harmonize the body, mind, and spirit. Each ritual is a step into the sacred, a dance with the divine, inviting us to attune our being to the higher vibrations and awaken the dormant potentials within.

Prayers in this bardo are the melodies of the heart, the whispering echoes of the soul calling out to the Infinite. They are the intimate conversations with the Divine, where we lay bare our deepest yearnings, fears, and aspirations. Through these heartfelt prayers, we cultivate a relationship with the unseen, recognizing the guiding hand of the divine in every moment of our existence.

The rituals and prayers become the vessel that navigates the turbulent waters of rebirth. They are the anchors that ground us in the midst of the swirling currents, providing stability and direction as we traverse the unknown. With every chant, every prostration, every offering, we are aligning our being with the cosmic order, drawing closer to the shores of enlightenment.

These practices are not about seeking external salvation; they are about the alchemy of transformation, the inner transmutation that turns the lead of ignorance into the gold of wisdom. It's about recognizing our divine nature, peeling away the layers of illusion, and revealing the radiant light of consciousness that shines within.

Central to all these practices is the cultivation of compassion, the recognition of the interconnectedness of all life. It's about seeing the other as a reflection of the self, understanding that our liberation is intrinsically linked to the liberation of all beings. Compassion becomes the guiding light, illuminating the path of selfless service and altruistic love.

Achieving a Favorable Rebirth

As the gentle winds of the Sidpa Bardo whisper tales of impermanence, the soul embarks on a journey towards rebirth, seeking harmony and the auspicious embrace of a new beginning. Achieving a favorable rebirth is both an art and a quest, guided by the interplay of karma, wisdom, and a heart steeped in compassion.

To navigate towards a favorable rebirth, one must first delve deep into karma. Every thought, word, and deed weaves a thread in this cosmic design, influencing the circumstances of rebirth. Embracing good deeds, altruistic intentions, and ethical living cultivates positive karma, guiding the soul towards a rebirth that reflects the beauty of one's spiritual journey.

By cultivating merit through acts of kindness, generosity, and selfless love, the soul attracts favorable conditions. The radiance of a compassionate heart reverberates through the bardo, harmonizing with the symphony of existence and opening the doors to a life filled with grace and spiritual enrichment.

The mind, in its luminous essence, holds another key to unlocking the gates of favorable rebirth. Meditating on the nature of mind, recognizing its innate purity and transient manifestations, the traveler transcends illusions. This profound realization enables the soul to rise above attachments and aversions, aligning with the divine flow of dharma and manifesting a rebirth that resonates with the highest aspirations.

Voicing prayers and aspirations for liberation is like planting seeds of light in the fertile grounds of the bardo. These heartfelt yearnings, imbued with the desire for enlightenment and the welfare of all beings, guide the soul towards a rebirth that nurtures spiritual growth. The echoes of these prayers weave a melody of liberation, attracting circumstances that facilitate the unfolding of one's spiritual potential.

In the dance of destiny within the Sidpa Bardo, turning to the wisdom of enlightened beings is a source of divine guidance. Invoking the blessings of Buddhas, Bodhisattvas, and spiritual guides, the soul is showered with light and insight. This sacred communion nurtures the spiritual seeds within, guiding the soul towards a rebirth that is a gateway to enlightenment and compassionate service.

Contemplating the transient nature of existence and the interconnectedness of all life forms shapes the soul's journey. This reflection fosters a deep appreciation for the preciousness of human rebirth and the opportunities it offers for spiritual growth. With this understanding, the soul navigates the bardo with wisdom, aligning with the cosmic dance and achieving a rebirth that is a canvas of limitless potential.

Chapter Four

Exploring the Lesser-Known Bardos

Introduction

In the Tibetan Book of the Dead, while the primary focus is laid upon the bardos of dying, death, and rebirth, there exists a substantial acknowledgment and exploration of the lesser-known bardos: Kyenay Bardo, Milam Bardo, and Samten Bardo. The text doesn't relegate these bardos to the periphery; rather, it introduces them purposefully, elucidating their integral roles in spiritual evolution.

The narrative within the text regarding these bardos is clear and deliberate, offering practitioners insights into their significance and functionality in the spiritual journey. The mention of Kyenay, Milam, and Samten Bardos is not cursory but is embedded with essential teachings and implications, indicative of their substantial roles in shaping consciousness and influencing spiritual progression.

The Tibetan Book of the Dead carefully structures the presentation of these bardos, providing readers with the necessary framework to comprehend their impact and relevance. It prompts an in-depth exploration of these states of existence, fostering a deeper understanding of their contributions to the spiritual journey.

In sum, the mention of these lesser-known bardos in the text is far from incidental. They are presented as fundamental elements of the spiritual narrative, each contributing uniquely to the comprehension and realization of the multifaceted nature of existence and consciousness.

Kyenay Bardo: The Bardo of This Life

In the intricate weave of Tibetan spirituality, the Kyenay Bardo emerges as a distinct strand, melding the ordinary with the extraordinary, the fleeting with the everlasting. This Bardo of This Life symbolizes our ongoing existence, a journey from the first breath to the last. Here, we are more than mere observers; we are the choreographers of our cosmic dance, the architects of our fate.

The Kyenay Bardo beckons us to embody mindfulness, to savor each heartbeat, each whisper of the wind. It's a clarion call to emerge from the shadows of unawareness, to acknowledge the ephemeral nature of the cosmos, and to nurture love and insight. Every thought, every flutter of the heart in this bardo, sows the seeds of our tomorrows, sculpting our karma and charting our passage through the ensuing bardos.

Navigating through the Kyenay Bardo, we dance with the myriad hues of human experience— the symphony of joy and the silence of sorrow, the warmth of love and the chill of absence, the bonds of attachment and the freedom of release. These aren't just random brushstrokes on the canvas of life; they are the colors that shape our spiritual evolution, revealing the fabric of reality, the unity in diversity, and the metamorphic potential of selfless love.

As we traverse the landscapes of Kyenay Bardo, we're guided to sow seeds of goodness, to embrace the rhythm of mindfulness, and to seek the wisdom hidden in the stars. The Dharma's luminous teachings light our way, sketching the roadmap to spiritual freedom. In the embrace of morality, the silence of meditation, and the depth of understanding, we build the pillars for a harmonious rebirth and the awakening of the soul.

Transience paints every scene in the Kyenay Bardo. All is fleeting, like a melody in the wind or a dream at dawn. In the dance with this truth, we untangle the strings of desire and resentment, fostering a spirit that flows like water, adapting and embracing the eternal dance of being.

Kyenay Bardo isn't a mere chapter to be leafed through; it's a sacred symphony, a melody of spiritual ascent. In the echoes of Buddha's wisdom, in the warmth of love, and in the unveiling of the cosmic dance, we find the rhythm to transform each beat of the heart into a step toward enlightenment.

At its core, the Kyenay Bardo sings of the sanctity of the now, a hymn inviting us to live with vigor, love with depth, and tread mindfully on enlightenment's path. It whispers the secrets of transformation in every rustle of the leaves, sees growth in every challenge, and finds in every breath, a dance with the divine.

Milam Bardo: The Bardo of Dream

Embarking on an exploration of the Milam Bardo, we find ourselves in a dreamscape where the line between the imaginary and the real is splendidly blurred. This is the realm of the Dream State, a landscape painted with the vibrant colors of our subconscious mind, where every nocturnal escapade holds the promise of self-discovery and revelation.

In the Milam Bardo, dreams serve as a dynamic mirror, reflecting the deepest corridors of our mind. These nocturnal narratives reveal the hidden crevices of our psyche, offering a unique perspective on our inherent nature and untapped potentials. By deciphering the symbols and themes within our dreams, we unearth invaluable insights and foster a profound connection with our inner selves.

Mastering the art of navigating the Milam Bardo is an endeavor of awakening within the dream. It is not about exerting control but about fostering awareness and discernment. Practices like lucid dreaming allow us to interact consciously with our dream environment, transforming each encounter into a step towards self-realization and spiritual refinement.

The dream state in Milam Bardo is rich with symbolism and metaphor. Every element within the dream, from the landscapes to the characters, holds symbolic meaning reflective of our thoughts, emotions, and experiences. Learning to interpret these symbols is a journey of uncovering the language of the subconscious mind and unlocking the mysteries of our inner world.

Milam Bardo offers a unique platform for experiencing higher states of consciousness. Through the conscious exploration of the dream state, we can access realms of existence beyond the physical, encounter spiritual guides, and receive teachings that resonate with the deepest truths of our being. This bardo serves as a bridge between the mundane and the divine, a gateway to realms untold.

The Bardo offers a canvas where the dreams painted by our subconscious minds become landscapes of exploration and discovery. It is a realm where every symbol holds a key to a deeper understanding of our true nature, and every night becomes an opportunity for spiritual advancement. By embracing the teachings of this bardo, we unlock the doors to realms within us, waiting to be explored.

Samten Bardo: The Bardo of Meditation

As we venture further into the diverse landscape of Tibetan spirituality, the Samten Bardo unravels before us as a realm of profound tranquility and meditative absorption. This is the Bardo of Meditation, a sanctuary where the external world fades away, leaving the mind to explore the boundless dimensions of its own nature.

In the embrace of Samten Bardo, we are summoned to transcend the superficial chatter of the mind, to let go of the transient shadows and tune into the symphony of silence within. This is a journey into the heart of stillness, where the flickering flames of desire and doubt are quenched, and the mind bathes in the serene light of awareness.

Navigating through Samten Bardo, we discover the subtle rhythms of our consciousness, the ebb and flow of thoughts, and the dance of sensations. Here, every moment is an invitation to delve deeper, to unravel the mysteries entwined within the tapestry of our being, and to witness the harmonious interplay of the cosmos.

The meditative sanctuary of Samten Bardo is not a retreat from the world but a deeper engagement with it. It is a space where the boundaries between self and other dissolve, where the heartbeat of the universe echoes within, and where compassion blooms like a lotus in the sunlit waters of the soul.

In this realm of meditation, we cultivate the art of mindful presence, attuning our senses to the whispering winds and the rustling leaves, feeling the interconnectedness of all life. It is a dance with the divine, a harmonious union of mind and cosmos, where we realize the inherent oneness of existence.

The teachings of Dharma illuminate our path in Samten Bardo, guiding us towards the realization of our innate wisdom and boundless love. With every breath, we are encouraged to embrace the impermanence of life, to let go of clinging, and to open our hearts to the infinite possibilities of the present moment.

Samten Bardo is a sacred symphony of inner peace and awakening. In this meditative sanctuary, we are not merely observers but active participants in the unfolding dance of existence. It is a journey of transformation, where every moment is a step towards enlightenment, and every breath is a whisper of the cosmic melody.

In essence, Samten Bardo is a celebration of the sacred stillness within, a reminder of the interconnected dance of life, and an invitation to embrace the boundless love and wisdom that resides in the heart of all beings. Here, in the serene embrace of meditation, we discover the true nature of reality and realize our potential for ultimate liberation.

Chapter Five

Historical Context

Origins and Discovery of the Text

Close your eyes for a moment and let your mind wander to Ancient Tibet, a mystic land of snow-capped peaks, serenading monastic chants, and vibrant prayer flags fluttering in the crisp mountain air.

Before Tibet was known in the West for its unique cuisine or political struggles, it stood as a beacon of spirituality and mysticism. In this serene landscape, the indigenous beliefs of Tibet thrived, creating a spiritual mosaic enriched with local deities and rituals. And amidst this spiritual dynamism, Buddhism, originating from the Indian subcontinent, made its way to the Tibetan plateau around the 7th century.

Buddhism's journey in Tibet wasn't that of a dominating force overtaking a landscape. Instead, it gently wove itself into the existing spiritual fabric, harmonizing with the ancient Bon religion and creating a synthesis of beliefs and practices.

Central to this melding of traditions was the realization of impermanence — the understanding that everything, from the seasons to life itself, is transient. Far from being a somber acknowledgment, this was a call to live with mindfulness, cherishing each moment and delving into the mysteries of existence.

This spiritual milieu set the stage for seminal texts like the "Bardo Thödol." Envision Tibetan monks and seekers, immersed in deep contemplation, their reflections magnified by the awe-inspiring vastness of the Himalayas.

The 8th century marked a transformative epoch in Tibet's spiritual tapestry. It was during this time that the enigmatic Padmasambhava, affectionately revered as Guru Rinpoche, graced the Tibetan plateau. The stories tell us that Guru Rinpoche was more than just a teacher. He was a beacon of transformative spiritual energy, intricately intertwining the deep tenets of Buddhism with the vibrant cultural mosaic of Tibet. He engaged with the community, debated profound truths, and even, as legends would have it, had some energetic interactions with the spirits of the land.

In the midst of these endeavors, Guru Rinpoche is believed to have composed and concealed several teachings, like spiritual messages in a bottle, meant for future seekers. Among these terma, or hidden treasures, was the "Bardo Thödol."

A few centuries later, this text was rediscovered by Terton Karma Lingpa. Think of him as the archaeologist of spiritual wisdom. And just like that, the "Bardo Thödol" was reintroduced to the world, ready to enlighten a new generation.

But here's a gentle note: Tibetan narratives beautifully blend history with legend. While we have these captivating tales of origin, the true essence of the "Bardo Thödol" is its timeless teachings and wisdom.

The Importance of the Text in Tibetan Funerary Practices

The cycle of life and death is a universal experience, but how we honor it varies across cultures and traditions. In the Tibetan landscape, where the majestic Himalayas meet the deep spirituality of its inhabitants, the passage from life to death is not merely an end. It's a transition, a journey. And guiding this journey is none other than the revered "Bardo Thödol."

In the heart of Tibetan communities, when a person nears their final moments, it is not uncommon for loved ones to gather around, reading aloud from the "Bardo Thödol." This is not just a ceremonial gesture. It's an act of compassion, a beacon of guidance for the departing soul as it embarks on the journey through the Bardos - those transitional states post-death and before rebirth.

But why is this text so pivotal in funerary practices? The answer lies in its profound teachings. The "Bardo Thödol" illuminates the path for the deceased, providing detailed accounts of what they might encounter and, most crucially, how to navigate these experiences. By reading it aloud, the living are imparting the wisdom and guidance the departed soul needs during this vulnerable transition.

Moreover, these recitations aren't exclusive to monastic settings or limited to the clergy. Laypeople, with sincere devotion, often engage in these readings, emphasizing the text's accessibility and universal importance in Tibetan culture. It's a collective endeavor of compassion, a community coming together to ensure that their departed are not alone, that they are armed with wisdom, and are guided toward a favorable rebirth.

While the West might turn to eulogies to celebrate a life passed, Tibetans harness the transformative power of the "Bardo Thödol" to guide the soul in its next adventure. It's a testament to the relationship Tibetans share with this text, intertwining deep spirituality with the raw human experience of loss, love, and hope.

The Journey from Oral Tradition to Written Manuscript

The ancient land of Tibet, with its deep spiritual roots, has always been a cradle for sacred stories and spiritual traditions. Such narratives, whether sung by firesides or whispered under the expansive starry skies, have been lullabies for the soul, echoing through the ages. Now, while the discovery and significance of texts like the "Bardo Thödol" were profound—thanks to Guru Rinpoche's concealed treasures—their true resonance lay in how they were passed down and preserved.

In the hallowed halls of monasteries, chants and rituals vibrated with age-old wisdom, echoing from one devoted monk to another. The "Bardo Thödol" itself, even before its written manuscript was reintroduced to the world, was part of this rich oral tradition. So, one might wonder, how did these orally transmitted chants and rituals from secluded Tibetan corners evolve into one of the most revered written manuscripts globally? The answer lies as much in the devotion of those who preserved it as in the wisdom it contained.

Oral tradition is an intricate art, where each word, each pause, each intonation is a deliberate choice, preserving the essence of the teachings. In ancient Tibet, many of these teachings and stories were not immediately committed to paper. Instead, they were meticulously memorized, recited, and passed down from master to disciple, from one generation to the next. This safeguarded the teachings from external threats and alterations, preserving their sanctity.

However, as centuries rolled on, the need to document this precious knowledge became apparent. The reason? Written manuscripts could be widely disseminated, ensuring that the teachings reached far and wide, untouched by the sands of time. Enter the scribes, those dedicated monks who would embark on the monumental task of transcribing these oral teachings onto paper, using the finest inks and most delicate brushes.

It is believed that the transcription of the "Bardo Thödol" was a monumental event. Imagine a serene monastery setting, where seasoned monks would recite the teachings, and the younger, eager scribes would diligently pen them down, ensuring that each phrase, each nuance was captured perfectly.

This transition from oral recitations to written manuscripts was not just a technical shift. It marked a pivotal moment in the preservation of the "Bardo Thödol." Now, the teachings were no longer confined to the memories of a select few. They were etched onto pages, ready to inspire countless generations, and ensuring that the wisdom within its folds would continue to guide souls on their spiritual journeys.

In essence, this journey from the spoken to the written word encapsulates the enduring spirit of the "Bardo Thödol." A testament to humanity's quest for knowledge and the tireless efforts of those dedicated to preserving it.

Yeshe Tsogyal: The Keeper of Teachings

Nestled within the tranquil folds of the Himalayas, as the sacred chants echoed through the monasteries and the teachings of the "Bardo Thödol" began to permeate Tibetan spiritual life, emerged a figure of unwavering devotion and spiritual brilliance — Yeshe Tsogyal. She wasn't just a whisper in the annals of Tibetan Buddhism; she was a symphony of wisdom, a principal consort of Guru Rinpoche, and a key transmitter of his teachings.

As we journey through the spiritual landscapes of Tibet, Yeshe Tsogyal's name is one that resonates with reverence and awe. Regarded as the Mother of Tibetan Buddhism, she bore the immense responsibility of safeguarding and transmitting the profound teachings bestowed by Guru Rinpoche. But who was Yeshe Tsogyal? And how did she become the Keeper of Teachings?

Born in the flowering valleys of Tibet, Yeshe Tsogyal's life was marked by spiritual awakening and divine encounters. Her journey with Guru Rinpoche was not just one of companionship but of profound spiritual partnership. Together, they delved into the mysteries of existence, explored the realms of consciousness, and unearthed the treasures of wisdom.

Yeshe Tsogyal's role was pivotal. She was the vessel that held the nectar of teachings, the scribe who etched wisdom into the consciousness of disciples, and the guide who navigated the seekers through the intricate paths of enlightenment. She absorbed the teachings of Guru Rinpoche with a heart full of devotion and a mind sharp with insight, ensuring that the sacred wisdom would endure through the sands of time.

The landscape of Tibet, with its rugged terrains and soaring peaks, mirrored the depth of Yeshe Tsogyal's spiritual journey. As she traversed this sacred land, disseminating the teachings of Guru Rinpoche, she encountered beings of all realms – humans seeking enlightenment, deities bestowing blessings, and spirits acknowledging the divine presence.

Her tales are not just narratives of a spiritual odyssey; they are reflections of her unwavering commitment to preserve the essence of the teachings. It is said that Yeshe Tsogyal concealed several of Guru Rinpoche's teachings as terma, ensuring that they would be discovered by destined Tertons in future generations. This act was not just about preservation; it was a testament to her foresight and understanding of the ever-evolving spiritual needs of humanity.

In the serene valleys and ancient monasteries of Tibet, where the prayers flags flutter in the wind and the chants fill the air, the legacy of Yeshe Tsogyal continues to thrive. Her life and contributions are celebrated, her teachings are revered, and her spiritual journey is a source of inspiration for both the novice seeker and the seasoned practitioner.

The Diverse Interpretations and Insights Offered by Tibetan Scholars

From the moment the ink dried on the first manuscript of the "Bardo Thödol," the text invited contemplation and exploration. It wasn't just a guide to the afterlife; it was a mirror reflecting the truths of existence, sparking a flame of inquiry within the hearts of Tibetan scholars.

Through the ages, these scholars have delved into the depths of the text, unraveling its layers and unveiling its insights. They've debated its teachings, explored its implications, and interpreted its wisdom, ensuring that the "Bardo Thödol" remains a living tradition of evolving understanding.

One such luminary is Longchenpa, a 14th-century Nyingma scholar, whose poetic writings and insights have illuminated the essence of the "Bardo Thödol." With a heart steeped in compassion and a mind sharp with wisdom, Longchenpa delved into the teachings of the text, unraveling its intricacies and bringing forth a tapestry of insights that continue to guide practitioners on the path to enlightenment.

The flickering butter lamps and the fragrant wafts of juniper incense set the stage as the teachings of the "Bardo Thödol" echo through the monastic halls. Here, amidst the rhythmic recitations and the contemplative silences, the monastic traditions play a pivotal role in preserving and propagating the teachings of the text.

Each monastery, with its unique lineage and traditions, serves as a cradle for the "Bardo Thödol," nurturing its teachings and ensuring their transmission to future generations. The monks, with their maroon robes and prayer beads, are not just the guardians of this sacred wisdom; they are the channels through which the teachings flow, reaching the hearts and minds of those who seek.

In the sacred spaces of these monasteries, the "Bardo Thödol" is not a static text but a dynamic tradition. It's explored through philosophical debates, meditated upon in the serene stillness, and lived through the daily practices of the monks. This vibrant monastic life ensures that the teachings of the "Bardo Thödol" are not confined to the ancient manuscripts but are woven into the very fabric of Tibetan spiritual life.

As we wander through the spiritual landscapes of Tibet, with the whispers of the ancient teachings in the air and the presence of luminaries like Yeshe Tsogyal and Longchenpa in the heart, the "Bardo Thödol" comes alive. It's not just a guide to the afterlife; it's a journey through the mysteries of existence, a dance of wisdom and compassion, and a living testament to the timeless heritage of Tibetan Buddhism.

The Evolution and Spread of Practices Related to the "Bardo Thödol"

As the golden rays of dawn paint the Himalayan skies and the harmonious hum of morning prayers fills the air, the spiritual legacy of the "Bardo Thödol" awakens in the hearts of practitioners across the ancient land of Tibet. Here, where the whispering winds carry tales of enlightenment and the rustling leaves sing the songs of sages, the practices related to the "Bardo Thödol" have evolved and spread like the petals of a lotus unfolding in the morning sun.

In the secluded valleys and serene plateaus of Tibet, the practices related to the "Bardo Thödol" found a fertile ground, nurturing the seeds of wisdom sown by the ancient teachings. With each passing season, these practices adapted to the rhythm of life in Tibetan communities, intertwining with local traditions and daily routines.

In the homes of the devout and the halls of the monasteries, the "Bardo Thödol" was not a text to be merely read; it was a lived experience, a guide to be contemplated and a wisdom to be embodied. The families gathered around the hearth, the elders imparting the teachings to the young, and the community coming together in times of transition—all were expressions of the living tradition of the "Bardo Thödol."

The evolution of these practices was not a linear journey but a dynamic dance, shaped by the diverse landscapes of Tibet and its spiritual heritage. From the tranquil meditation caves of the Himalayas to the bustling marketplaces of Lhasa, the "Bardo Thödol" found its expression in myriad forms, each reflecting the unique flavor of the local community.

With the gentle caress of the mountain breeze and the tireless steps of devoted pilgrims, the teachings of the "Bardo Thödol" began their journey beyond the rugged terrains of Tibet. Like the flowing rivers that carve their paths through the mountains, the wisdom of the "Bardo Thödol" touched new shores, quenching the spiritual thirst of seekers across borders.

As the teachings traveled, they encountered new cultures, diverse traditions, and varied perspectives. Each encounter was a confluence, a meeting of minds and hearts, where the timeless wisdom of the "Bardo Thödol" melded with the unique insights of different lands.

In these foreign soils, the practices related to the "Bardo Thödol" evolved and adapted, taking on new forms and expressions. They found a home in the quiet meditation halls of Japan, resonated with the contemplative chants of Thai monasteries, and echoed in the scholarly debates of Indian ashrams.

This journey was not just a geographical expansion; it was a spiritual blossoming. The "Bardo Thödol" was no longer confined to the land of its origin; it became a global heritage, a beacon of light guiding humanity on the path to awakening.

As we traverse the spiritual landscapes shaped by the "Bardo Thödol," witnessing its evolution and spread, we are reminded that this sacred text is not a relic of the past but a living tradition. It's a dance of wisdom and compassion that continues to unfold, inspiring hearts, enlightening minds, and guiding souls on their journey through the mysteries of existence.

Whether nestled in the serene valleys of Tibet or resonating in the bustling cities across the globe, the teachings of the "Bardo Thödol" remain a timeless source of inspiration and guidance, inviting us all to join the dance and embark on the path to enlightenment.

The Debate on the Authenticity and Origins of the Text

In the world of religious studies, the Bardo Thödol holds a place of both reverence and intrigue. The text's intricate teachings on life, death, and rebirth has inspired countless on their spiritual journey, yet its origins and authenticity have sparked debates, casting shadows of mystery around it.

The narrative of concealment and discovery has raised eyebrows among scholars and historians. Some question the historical accuracy of this account, proposing alternative theories about the text's creation and its lineage of transmission.

The debate around the authenticity of the Bardo Thödol stems from various angles – historical, literary, and doctrinal. Scholars dissect the linguistic style, doctrinal content, and historical context, seeking to uncover the layers of its origin and establish its authenticity.

Some argue that discrepancies in style and content point to multiple authors over different periods, while others uphold the traditional narrative, attributing the work to the singular vision of Padmasambhava and the subsequent revelation by Karma Lingpa.

While the quest for the Bardo Thödol's historical truth continues, the impact of the debate is multifold. It invites reflection on the nature of religious authenticity and the ways in which sacred texts are valued, interpreted, and preserved. Moreover, it challenges practitioners and scholars alike to consider the significance of the text's teachings, regardless of its historical origins.

Its Impact on Tibetan Society and Rituals

The Bardo Thödol, with its profound teachings and vivid imagery, has woven itself into the very fabric of Tibetan society, shaping the spiritual landscapes and influencing the ritualistic practices of the people. Its echoes can be heard in the chants of the monks, seen in the thangkas adorning the monasteries, and felt in the daily lives of the devout.

In the rugged terrains of Tibet, where the boundaries between the earthly and the divine often blur, the Bardo Thödol serves as a spiritual navigator, guiding souls through the transitionary states of death and rebirth. It's not just a text; it's a companion for the departed, a source of solace for the grieving, and a map for those traversing the spiritual path.

The recitation of the Bardo Thödol at deathbeds is a common practice, believed to assist the deceased in recognizing the nature of their mind and reality, thereby aiding them in attaining a favorable rebirth or enlightenment.

The impact of the Bardo Thödol is especially pronounced in the rituals and ceremonies centered around death and dying. It shapes the way Tibetans approach death, perceive the afterlife, and perform funeral rites. The text has given rise to a multitude of ritualistic practices, each imbued with symbolic meanings and spiritual significance.

These rituals, often led by spiritual leaders or family members, are designed to honor the deceased, support their journey through the bardos, and cultivate merit for both the living and the departed.

Beyond the realms of death and rebirth, the Bardo Thödol also serves as an ethical and moral compass for the living. Its teachings on karma, impermanence, and compassion influence the ethical framework of Tibetan society, shaping values, informing moral choices, and inspiring acts of kindness and generosity.

The cultural imprint of the Bardo Thödol is visible in various forms of Tibetan art, music, and literature. The vivid descriptions of the bardos, deities, and realms have inspired a mosaic of artistic expressions, encapsulating the essence of the text in colors, sounds, and words.

Chapter Six

Guiding the Departed

Introduction

Guidance through the bardos is a journey steeped in compassion and deep understanding. It's a path that requires us, the living, to step into realms of consciousness that echo with ancient wisdom and sacred resonance. This chapter, dear reader, is an invitation to explore the pivotal role we play in assisting the departed souls as they traverse the labyrinthine realms of the bardos.

The Tibetan Book of the Dead speaks volumes about the interconnectedness of all beings and the boundless nature of compassion. It is compassion that forms the foundation of every practice and ritual designed to assist the departed. To set a compassionate tone is to create an atmosphere brimming with love, understanding, and a deep wish for the welfare of the departed. It is about invoking the boundless love that resides within each of us and directing it towards the soul making its way through the bardos.

As we chant, meditate, and perform rituals, our intentions should be clear and pure. It is not merely about the recitation of verses or the enactment of rituals; it is about infusing each word, each action with genuine love and compassion. It is about creating a beacon of light that guides the departed through the often tumultuous journey, ensuring they are not alone, but accompanied by the warmth of our hearts.

In the bardo journey, the living are not mere observers. We are active participants, guides in a terrain marked by its ephemeral and illusory nature. Our role is to provide support, to be the anchor in a sea of change, and to radiate the love and compassion that can illuminate the path for the departed.

The Bardo Thödol outlines various methods and practices that the living can employ to aid the deceased. These range from chanting specific verses, performing dedicated rituals, to maintaining a serene and positive environment around the physical remains. Each practice is a testament to the profound understanding of life, death, and rebirth that the Tibetan Book of the Dead encapsulates.

Reading the Bardo Thödol to the Deceased

In the hushed tones of reverence and the gentle cadence of ancient verses, the reading of the Bardo Thödol opens a sacred dialogue between the realms of the living and the departed. It is more than an act of remembrance; it is a beacon of light guiding the deceased through the unknown, a harmonious symphony echoing through the bardos.

Reading The Bardo Thödol to the deceased is a practice of paramount significance, as it offers guidance, reassurance, and clarity during their journey through the bardos. Timing holds a sacred essence in this practice. The teachings of the Bardo Thödol are most impactful when the deceased is in a receptive state, navigating through the uncertainties and revelations of the bardos. Discerning the opportune moments to read the verses requires attunement to the subtle energies and a deep understanding of the teachings embodied in the text.

The initial readings commence shortly after death, as the consciousness of the deceased is believed to be in a state of heightened awareness and receptivity.

Subsequent readings are timed with the transitions between the bardos, aligning with the pivotal moments of realization and potential liberation for the deceased.

The verses of the Bardo Thödol are imbued with teachings that illuminate the nature of mind, revealing the intrinsic purity and luminosity of consciousness. As the reader's voice resonates through the silent realms, the deceased is encouraged to recognize the essence of their own mind, to glimpse the radiant clarity that lies beneath the veil of illusions.

This recognition is pivotal, as it holds the potential to liberate the deceased from the cycle of rebirth and guide them toward enlightenment. The teachings emphasize the interconnectedness of all beings, the transient nature of reality, and the boundless compassion that permeates existence.

The reader, in articulating the verses, serves as a guide, gently steering the deceased towards these profound realizations. The practice is not merely a recitation of words but a heartfelt offering of guidance, a manifestation of the universal bond of love and compassion that unites all beings.

In this sacred exchange, the reader and the deceased embark on a journey of mutual transformation. The teachings of the Bardo Thödol are not only a guiding light for the deceased but also a source of inspiration and insight for the living. As the verses of the Bardo Thödol echo through the realms of the bardos, they weave together wisdom, love, and liberation. The deceased, guided by the teachings, are offered a path towards recognition of their true nature, and the living, in turn, are invited to reflect on the truths revealed in the sacred text. This harmonious dance of guidance and realization embodies the essence of the Bardo Thödol.

Prayers, Chants, and Protective Invocations

Within the mystical pages of the Tibetan Book of the Dead lies a symphony of prayers, chants, and invocations. Each serves as a guiding light, directing departed souls through the labyrinth of the bardos. In this subchapter, we'll unravel the essence of these spiritual harmonies, examining their significance, meanings, and the potent energies they introduce to the journey of the deceased.

In Tibetan Buddhism, every prayer is a thread of divine wisdom, a melody of compassion, echoing through the transient and the eternal. The prayers are not mere words; they are the embodiment of enlightened intentions, resonating with the energies of love, guidance, and protection.

One such prayer, the revered Om Mani Padme Hum, is a kaleidoscope of spiritual vibrations, each syllable a facet of divine wisdom and compassionate energy. It is a guiding light in the realms of the bardos, a reminder of the inherent Buddha-nature within every being, and a pathway leading to enlightenment and liberation.

The Amitabha Buddha Pure Land Prayer is another spiritual gem, carrying the aspirations and blessings for rebirth in the Pure Land, a realm of unbounded compassion and enlightened wisdom. It is a spiritual embrace, enveloping the departed in a cocoon of divine grace and guiding them towards the shores of awakening.

These are but glimpses into the vast repository of prayers within the Tibetan tradition, each with a unique essence and purpose, serving as anchors and guides through the ever-shifting landscapes of existence.

The practice of invoking positive influences is akin to crafting a sanctuary of light in the midst of the bardos. By calling upon the benevolent deities, the guardians of the Dharma, and the Bodhisattvas of compassion, we surround the departed with a protective aura of divine energy, shielding them from the shadows and guiding them towards the dawn of enlightenment.

This is not a passive act; it is an engagement of the heart and spirit, a weaving of spiritual resilience and strength, ensuring that the journey through the bardos is marked by clarity, wisdom, and the loving presence of the enlightened ones.

Warding off negativity is not an act of exclusion; it is a cultivation of spiritual fortitude, a building of inner light that dispels the darkness and allows the teachings of the Bardo Thödol to be absorbed with an open heart and a clear mind.

Making Offerings and Virtuous Acts

Embarking further on the spiritual path laid out in the Tibetan Book of the Dead, we find ourselves in the presence of profound practices, those of making offerings and performing virtuous acts. These practices are not mere rituals; they are imbued with deep intentions and loving kindness, reverberating through the bardos and extending a helping hand to the deceased.

In the heart of Tibetan Buddhism lies the precious gem of generosity. It's not just a physical act of giving; it's a spiritual cultivation of selflessness, an open-handedness that extends beyond materiality and touches the essence of our being. The practice of generosity is a rain of blessings, nurturing the seeds of compassion and wisdom both in the giver and the receiver.

Making offerings in the context of guiding the departed is a dance of love and letting go. It's about offering the best of what we have, be it food, flowers, light, or incense, with a heart full of love and a spirit untainted by attachment. The offerings become a bridge of light, connecting the living with the deceased, and creating a channel for blessings and positive energies to flow.

This practice is not confined to the temple or the altar; it is a way of life, a continuous flow of giving and receiving, acknowledging the interdependence of all beings and the boundless nature of compassion.

Equally vital in guiding the departed is the practice of generating merit. Merit, in the Buddhist context, is the positive energy accumulated through virtuous acts, acts that are aligned with Dharma and emanate from a place of love, wisdom, and compassion. Every act of kindness, every word of truth, every moment of mindfulness, contributes to this pool of merit.

For the deceased navigating the bardos, this generated merit becomes a beacon of light, illuminating their path and dispelling the shadows of confusion and fear. It's an offering of spiritual sustenance, nourishing their journey towards rebirth or enlightenment.

By dedicating the merit generated through our virtuous acts to the deceased, we are not merely sending good wishes; we are actively participating in their journey, sharing our spiritual wealth, and contributing to their well-being and awakening.

The Power of Meditation and Compassionate Intention

The journey through the bardos is shrouded in mystery and uncertainty, where the deceased might encounter both enlightenment and illusion. Being anchored in mindfulness and cultivating a supportive presence become the anchors amidst this shifting sea. Mindfulness is not a passive observation; it is an active engagement with the present moment, a harmonious tuning of the heart and mind to the symphony of existence.

By practicing mindfulness, we develop a clarity of perception and a depth of understanding, enabling us to be truly present for the deceased. We become the steady ground, the compassionate witness to their journey, reflecting back the light of awareness and the warmth of loving-kindness.

In this supportive presence, we don't just observe; we respond. We respond with empathy, with understanding, and with a deep, unshakeable love that transcends the boundaries of life and death. This presence becomes a sanctuary, a haven of peace and solace for the departed.

The heart of compassionate intention is the art of directing positive energy. It's about channeling the boundless love and wisdom within us towards the deceased, enveloping them in a cocoon of light and love. Every thought of goodwill, every intention of well-being, becomes a ripple in the ocean of consciousness, reaching the shores of the deceased's experience.

This directed positive energy is not just a transient wave; it's a transformative force, shaping the landscapes of the bardos, clearing the fog of confusion, and lighting up the path towards liberation. It's a testament to the interconnectedness of all beings, to the universal nature of love, and to the boundless potential of the human spirit.

Navigating the 49-Day Period

The 49-day period following death holds a place of significant prominence. This duration is not just a measure of time; it is a sacred canvas on which the journey of the deceased unfolds, a framework that offers both challenges and opportunities for growth and liberation.

To navigate this sacred time frame is to understand its rhythm, its ebb and flow. Each of the seven weeks represents a unique phase in the journey through the bardos, a delicate dance between the realms of the known and the unknown, the manifest and the unmanifest. The Tibetan Book of the Dead guides us with a gentle hand through this intricate labyrinth, shedding light on the mysteries that await and the milestones that mark the path.

Recognizing the significance of each phase within the 7-week period is akin to attuning ourselves to the heartbeat of the bardo journey. It's about being present, being receptive, and being responsive to the subtle nuances and profound transformations that characterize this sacred passage.

The initial week is characterized by a dawning realization of death. The deceased grapples with an array of emotions, amidst the unfamiliar and transient nature of the Bardo. The Tibetan Book of the Dead provides essential teachings and prayers, emphasizing the impermanent nature of this state and aiding the deceased in moving past fear and confusion. For the living, it's a period of profound connection and expression of love and gratitude, establishing a supportive spiritual foundation for the journey ahead.

Entering the second week, the deceased becomes more attuned to the Bardo's landscapes, encountering various manifestations. The text guides them in discerning between illusion and reality, encouraging a balanced perspective and avoiding attachment or aversion. The living continue their supportive practices, adapting to the evolving needs of the deceased, and fostering an environment of understanding and acceptance.

The third week brings forth vivid karmic visions and reflections. The deceased faces the consequences of past actions and begins to comprehend the intricate web of karma. The teachings offer insights on navigating through these revelations, fostering a mindset of responsibility and equanimity. The living, in turn, focus on practices that generate positive energy and merit, aiding the deceased in addressing karmic patterns with wisdom.

As the fourth week unfolds, the potential for liberation becomes more prominent. The deceased is guided to recognize the luminosity of their inherent nature and the possibility of breaking free from the cycle of birth and death. The living intensify their meditative practices and compassionate intentions, channeling positive energy to support the deceased in realizing this pivotal opportunity.

In the fifth week, there's a deepening of insight and wisdom for the deceased. The teachings elucidate the interconnectedness of all phenomena and the essence of emptiness. The deceased is encouraged to cultivate an understanding of the nature of mind and reality, moving closer to liberation. The living engage in reflective practices, contemplating the teachings' profundity and directing thoughts of enlightenment towards the deceased.

The penultimate week is marked by final preparations and resolutions. The deceased revisits the experiences of the preceding weeks, consolidating insights and making essential decisions regarding the future. The text provides guidance on evaluating different rebirth realms and making informed choices based on wisdom and merit. The living concentrate on generating positive influences, aligning their intentions with the deceased's aspirations.

In the final week, the deceased is at the crossroads of rebirth or liberation. The teachings in the Tibetan Book of the Dead come to fruition, guiding the deceased in making the ultimate transition based on their accumulated wisdom and merits. The living maintain a steady flow of supportive energy, reinforcing the deceased's resolve and aspirations, and offering prayers for a favorable rebirth or attainment of liberation.

Adapting Practices to Individual Journeys

In guiding a soul through the Bardo, recognizing the uniqueness of each journey is pivotal. The landscapes of the Bardo might be similar, but the experiences, visions, and revelations encountered by the deceased are distinctly shaped by their individual karma and consciousness. Thus, the teachings of the Tibetan Book of the Dead are not one-size-fits-all; they are a foundation, a starting point that requires adaptability and a discerning application based on the specific needs of the deceased.

Start by assessing the spiritual inclinations, characteristics, and past experiences of the deceased. This initial understanding forms the bedrock upon which personalized guidance can be molded. It's not just about reciting prayers and meditations; it's about modifying and directing them to address the unique challenges and needs that unfold. Tailoring these practices enhances their effectiveness, making the spiritual support more resonant and meaningful for the deceased.

Flexibility and responsiveness are paramount. The Bardo experience is fluid, and as such, our approach should mirror this dynamism. Being steadfast in tradition is valuable, but there's also a need for innovation in applying the teachings. Balancing the old with the new ensures that the practices remain relevant and impactful, providing the deceased with the most apt guidance.

Regular observation and reflection on the deceased's progress are crucial. This mindfulness fosters a deeper connection, allowing the living to stay attuned to the shifts in the journey and to adjust their support accordingly. It's not merely about following a script; it's about being present, being responsive, and cultivating insight and wisdom suited to the individual's experiences within the Bardo.

In essence, adapting practices to individual journeys is an exercise in deep compassion and understanding. It's about honoring the individuality of each soul, ensuring that the profound teachings of the Tibetan Book of the Dead are not just recited but are lived, experienced, and applied in the most beneficial and meaningful way possible.

Chapter Seven

Comparison with Related Texts

Kangyur and Tengyur

Within Tibetan Buddhist literature, the Bardo Thödol, Kangyur, and Tengyur each hold distinctive places, serving varied yet interconnected roles in illuminating the path of Dharma. Comparing these revered texts unveils their complementary nature, revealing a harmonious blend of foundational teachings, insightful commentaries, and practical guidance for both life and the afterlife.

The Kangyur, regarded as the cornerstone of Tibetan Buddhist scripture, is the sacred reservoir of the Buddha's teachings. Encompassing sutras, tantras, and Vinaya texts, it lays the very bedrock of Buddhist philosophy, ethics, and metaphysical insights. This extensive compilation serves as the source of wisdom, from which the rivers of understanding flow, nourishing the spiritual landscapes of practitioners and scholars alike.

Building upon the foundational teachings of the Kangyur, the Tengyur provides a rich layer of interpretation and analysis by esteemed Indian and Tibetan scholars. It's akin to a guiding light, illuminating the nuances of the Buddha's teachings, unraveling their depth, and aiding practitioners in assimilating and actualizing the Dharma in their lives. The Tengyur not only clarifies but also contextualizes, making the timeless wisdom of the Buddha accessible and relevant across epochs.

While each text holds its unique essence, there's an intrinsic interplay between them. The Bardo Thödol, despite its specialized focus, is deeply rooted in the principles enshrined in the Kangyur and is enriched by the philosophical insights elucidated in the Tengyur. The concepts of impermanence, karma, compassion, and the nature of mind are threads that weave through all three, creating a harmonious wisdom.

The Bardo Thödol's emphasis on recognizing the innate Buddha-nature and the luminosity of the mind during transitional states echoes the foundational teachings of the Kangyur and finds resonance with the analytical depth of the Tengyur. However, the Bardo Thödol stands apart in its application of these principles to the unique challenges and opportunities presented by the bardos, offering a roadmap to liberation that is both immediate and profoundly transformative.

Guhya-samāja Tantra

The Guhya-samāja Tantra, translating to the "Secret Assembly Tantra", is a work within the esoteric world of Tibetan Tantric Buddhism. It unravels the mysteries of divine union, transformation, and the multifaceted interplay between form and emptiness, shedding light on the advanced practices aimed at achieving Buddhahood within a single lifetime. Known for its teachings on the subtle body, channels, winds, and drops, this Tantra is a guide to inner alchemy, where the practitioner engages with divine energies and consciousness to realize the innate Buddha-nature.

The Bardo Thödol, with its vivid depictions of the bardos and practical guidance for the deceased, offers a transformative journey through the intermediate states, emphasizing the recognition of one's innate Buddha-nature and the potential for liberation. In contrast, the Guhya-samāja Tantra delves into the esoteric practices of deity yoga, mandala visualization, and subtle body energies, guiding the adept towards the realization of the union of bliss and emptiness.

Venturing into the depths of these two texts, we discover a dance of similarities and variations. Both are imbued with the wisdom of Vajrayana, an integral path of Tibetan Buddhism, where the practitioner endeavors to perceive the inseparability of bliss and emptiness, samsara and nirvana. The Bardo Thödol and the Guhya-samāja Tantra, in their unique ways, offer insights and methods to recognize and realize the nature of mind and reality, albeit through different lenses and applications.

While both texts lead the practitioner towards the summit of enlightenment, they offer distinctive paths. The Guhya-samāja Tantra is a meticulous map to the inner cosmos, demanding adeptness, initiation, and unwavering commitment to navigate the intricate terrains of Tantra.

Yet, within their diversity, a harmonious resonance emerges. The teachings on the nature of mind, compassion, and wisdom are foundational stones in both texts, reflecting the interconnectedness and unity of the Tibetan Buddhist tradition. The Guhya-samāja Tantra's emphasis on transformation and union finds a complementary echo in the Bardo Thödol's guidance on recognizing and seizing the luminous opportunities presented in the bardos.

Lamrim Chenmo

The Lamrim Chenmo embodies a systematic approach to spiritual cultivation, offering a structured path that encompasses the entirety of the Buddha's teachings. With its roots in the teachings of Atiśa, this text is like a detailed map that guides practitioners from the very beginning of the path, through intermediate stages, and ultimately to the pinnacle of Vajrayana practices. The teachings are presented in a graded manner, allowing the practitioner to cultivate renunciation, bodhicitta, and the correct view of emptiness, progressively deepening their realization of the Dharma.

Both Bardo Thödol and Lamrim Chenmo share striking similarities in their core themes. They highlight life's impermanence, the crucial role of ethical conduct, and the transformative power of compassion and wisdom. Central concepts like karma, rebirth, and liberation are consistently interwoven in their teachings.

However, a divergence in focus and application becomes evident as we delve deeper. The Lamrim Chenmo offers a panoramic view of the spiritual path, addressing practitioners across the spectrum of development and guiding them through the progressive stages of the path to enlightenment. The Bardo Thödol is a specialized manual for a crucial juncture of existence, whereas Lamrim Chenmo is a comprehensive guide to living a spiritual life.

The comparison reveals how these texts, while distinct in their approach and emphasis, serve as complementary facets of the Dharma jewel. The Bardo Thödol illuminates the possibilities of liberation inherent in every moment, especially during the transition between life and death. In contrast, Lamrim Chenmo lays out a detailed and structured path, ensuring that practitioners cultivate the necessary qualities and realizations in a sequential and balanced manner.

Dzogchen Texts

Dzogchen teachings unfold as a radiant symphony, inviting practitioners to realize the primordially pure nature of the mind. This path emphasizes direct experience over intellectual analysis, inviting us into an immediate recognition of our innate Buddha-nature. The texts of Dzogchen are like melodies that guide us beyond conceptual boundaries, revealing the boundless sky of awareness, where the clouds of dualistic perception dissolve into luminous clarity.

In their essence, the Bardo Thödol and Dzogchen texts share a harmonious tune — they both illuminate the transformative potential inherent in each moment and guide us toward liberation from the cycle of existence. Both teach the practitioner to recognize and utilize the natural luminosity of the mind, especially during transitions and moments of uncertainty.

However, the expressions of these teachings are as diverse as the myriad reflections of the moon in water. The Bardo Thödol, with its vivid imagery and detailed guidance, is like a meticulously composed symphony, guiding the practitioner through the various stages of the bardo with precision and clarity. It offers a path through the labyrinth of the intermediate states, turning each moment of confusion into an opportunity for awakening.

Conversely, Dzogchen texts are like free-flowing improvisations, emphasizing the spontaneity and effortlessness of recognizing the natural state. They invite us to let go of striving and to rest in the simplicity of being, where enlightenment is not something to be achieved, but realized as always present.

The Bardo Thödol holds a unique place in the vast landscape of Tibetan literature and teachings. It serves as a bridge between the various schools of Tibetan Buddhism, its vivid descriptions of the bardo experiences and its practical advice make it a valuable companion for those traversing the uncertain terrains of death and rebirth.

In contrast, Dzogchen texts represent the pinnacle of spiritual realization in the Nyingma tradition. Their emphasis on the direct and immediate recognition of the nature of mind makes them a profound and transformative path, suitable for those with the capacity for higher insight and realization.

Jataka Tales

The Jataka Tales are akin to vibrant tapestries depicting the myriad lives of the Buddha, unraveling moral and ethical guidance through enchanting stories. These tales are imbued with the essence of compassion, generosity, and wisdom, serving as illustrative parables to inspire ethical living and spiritual awakening. Each story is a reflection of the Buddha's journey, showcasing the cultivation of virtues that lead to enlightenment.

Comparing the Bardo Thödol and the Jataka Tales is like listening to the ethereal echoes of celestial realms intertwining with the hearty tunes of the earth. The Jataka Tales, with their earthly resonance, focus on the cultivation of virtues and ethical conduct in the human realm. These tales, with their colorful characters and captivating narratives, provide practical lessons on kindness, integrity, and selflessness, laying the foundation for spiritual growth and awakening.

Despite their divergent focus, a harmonious undercurrent connects the Bardo Thödol and the Jataka Tales. The Bardo Thödol's transcendental wisdom on navigating the bardos complements the ethical grounding provided by the Jataka Tales. The tales, with their emphasis on virtuous living, sow the seeds of compassion and wisdom that blossom into the profound understanding of the nature of existence, as elucidated in the Bardo Thödol.

The Bardo Thödol and the Jataka Tales represent distinctive threads woven into the Buddhist teachings. The Bardo Thödol serves as a beacon of light guiding the way through the unknown, its teachings resonating with the mysteries of life, death, and rebirth. The Jataka Tales, on the other hand, are like the vibrant colors and patterns that adorn the fabric of everyday life, teaching us to live with kindness, generosity, and wisdom.

Together, these teachings create a harmonious symphony, inviting us to dance to the rhythms of ethical living and transcendent understanding. They beckon us to embrace the earthly and the ethereal, to live with compassion and to traverse the bardos with awareness, discovering the luminous essence of our being in the wondrous journey of awakening.

Lojong Texts

With their origin rooted in the Tibetan tradition, Lojong or "mind training" texts are like cherished manuals for navigating the landscape of life with an open heart and a lucid mind. These texts present a series of aphorisms and practices designed to awaken bodhicitta—the enlightened heart of compassion—and to purify the mind from afflictive emotions. Through a harmonious blend of wisdom and compassion, the Lojong teachings encourage us to view adversities as opportunities for growth and to cultivate love and understanding in every encounter.

On the surface, the Bardo Thödol and the Lojong texts may seem like different chapters in the spiritual narrative, but they share a harmonious connection in their essence. The Bardo Thödol, with its ethereal guidance through the realms of existence, and the Lojong texts, with their grounding principles on mind transformation, together weave a tapestry that portrays the dance between transcendent wisdom and immanent compassion.

The Lojong teachings provide practical tools for transforming the mind and heart in the midst of daily challenges, enabling us to face the impermanence and interdependence of life with equanimity and grace. The unity in diversity between the Bardo Thödol and the Lojong texts is like a symphony where different instruments create a harmonious melody. While the Bardo Thödol unveils the luminosity of the mind in the transitional states, the Lojong texts shine a light on the path of altruistic living and mental clarity in the here and now.

Both texts, in their unique ways, guide us towards realizing the non-dual nature of reality and embodying compassion for all beings. The teachings of the Bardo Thödol and Lojong converge in their aspiration to liberate beings from suffering and to unveil the innate wisdom and love that lie within the heart of every individual.

Blue Annals

The Blue Annals stands as a monumental work, a historical chronicle meticulously penned by Gö Lotsawa Zhönnu Pel in the 15th century. This illustrious text threads together Tibetan Buddhism, chronicling the lives, teachings, and lineages of eminent spiritual masters and schools of Tibetan Buddhism. The Blue Annals opens a window to the spiritual heritage of Tibet, offering a glimpse into the historical unfolding of Dharma in the Land of Snows.

At the meeting point of these two revered texts, a symphony of teachings and histories unravels. The Bardo Thödol resonates with the timeless echoes of the Blue Annals' narratives of spiritual masters, their teachings, challenges, and triumphs. While the Bardo Thödol is a guide to the inner realms of the mind and spirit, the Blue Annals is a journey through the rivers of time, reflecting the external blossoming of Dharma in the Tibetan landscape.

The paths of the Bardo Thödol and the Blue Annals diverge in form and content, yet converge in the boundless wisdom they embody. The Blue Annals weave the collective story of Tibetan Buddhism, shedding light on the diversity, resilience, and richness of the various spiritual traditions and lineages.

In their convergence, the texts offer a holistic view of the Dharma, complementing the individual journey of awakening with the collective heritage of spiritual wisdom. They invite us to explore the inner landscapes of the mind and the outer terrains of spiritual history, guiding us towards a deeper appreciation of the multifaceted gem of Tibetan Buddhism.

Comparing the Bardo Thödol and the Blue Annals, we find a confluence where consciousness intertwines with the historical narratives of Tibetan Buddhism.

The teachings of the Bardo Thödol, complemented by the stories from the Blue Annals, form a union of wisdom, urging us to delve into our inner selves and appreciate the vast spiritual legacy of Tibet.

The Egyptian Book of the Dead

In the realm of ancient wisdom, two luminous texts, the Egyptian Book of the Dead and the Bardo Thödol, offer profound insights into the mysteries of life, death, and the beyond. While the two texts originate from diverse cultures and spiritual traditions, present a harmonious interplay of philosophical depth and cosmological richness, guiding us through the intricate pathways of the human soul's journey.

Embarking on a journey through ancient Egypt, we encounter a philosophy deeply intertwined with Ma'at, the embodiment of truth, order, balance, and morality. The Egyptian Book of the Dead serves as a vessel, guiding the soul through landscapes where devotion to gods, moral conduct, and harmony with the natural and divine order resonate at every step. The myriad spells and invocations depict a worldview where maintaining cosmic and social balance is not just pivotal, but essential, influencing the soul's journey in the afterlife.

The core principles of Ma'at echo through the ages, emphasizing truthfulness, justice, and harmony, resonating with the ethical teachings of compassion and mindfulness. This convergence of ethical living and spiritual realization becomes a common thread, weaving through the fabric of both texts, illuminating the path toward enlightenment and a harmonious afterlife.

While the Egyptian Book of the Dead anchors the soul in devotion, ritual, and moral integrity, the Bardo Thödol offers insights into the fluidity of existence, the interconnectedness of all beings, and the transformative power of wisdom and compassion. These divergent pathways reveal the multifaceted nature of human spirituality, each offering insights, reflections, and avenues towards truth, harmony, and transcendence.

Exploring these philosophical dimensions, we're invited to a contemplative dance with existence, the cosmos, and the human spirit. The dialogues between these texts enrich our understanding of life, death, and the profound quest for meaning, weaving a tapestry that transcends temporal and spatial boundaries.

Diving into the cosmology of the Egyptian Book of the Dead, we visualize a vibrant realm where the soul, or Ba, embarks on a transformative journey through the Duat, encountering divine judges and navigating landscapes symbolic of moral integrity and the balance of Ma'at. This journey reaches a crescendo in the Weighing of the Heart ceremony, a divine reckoning determining the soul's harmonious alignment with the cosmic order and its passage to the Field of Reeds.

Parallel to this, the cosmological framework of the Bardo Thödol unfolds a dynamic universe, where the journey through various bardos offers moments of liberation for those who recognize the luminosity of the Dharmakaya, while others continue the cyclic dance of Samsara. The narratives of transition, transformation, and moral reckoning shared by both texts illuminate the intricacies of the afterlife and underscore the significance of moral living and spiritual understanding.

The narratives converge as we explore the soul's journey, depicted as a transformative process where past actions, intentions, and understanding shape the individual's destiny. In the Egyptian tradition, the journey involves external judgment, adherence to cosmic order, and seeking the favor of deities, symbolized by the trials in the Duat and the ultimate union with the divine.

Contrastingly, the Bardo Thödol encapsulates a journey of internal realization and awakening, where confronting one's own mind and karma reveals the potential for enlightenment and liberation. Despite the differences in approach, universal themes of reflection, redemption, and renewal emerge, highlighting the timeless human quest for meaning, harmony, and transcendence.

Chapter Eight

Philosophical and Spiritual Insights

The Nature of Reality

Reality, as depicted in the Bardo Thödol, is not a linear, tangible entity but a dynamic interplay of illusion and truth. The text introduces us to a reality that is illusory, likened to a dream, a mirage, or the reflections of the moon on water. It invites readers to look beyond the apparent and perceive the ephemeral nature of the world, where phenomena are transient and devoid of inherent existence.

This is not a nihilistic view but a transformative realization. By understanding the illusory nature of reality, we begin to discern the ultimate truth—emptiness. Emptiness in Buddhism doesn't imply non-existence but denotes the absence of inherent nature in all phenomena, leading to the understanding that everything is interconnected and interdependent.

The Tibetan Book of the Dead unveils the concept of dependent origination, which is the heartbeat of Buddhist philosophy. This principle elucidates that all phenomena arise, exist, and cease due to the intricate web of causes and conditions. Nothing exists in isolation; everything is a nexus of relationships, a harmonious dance of interdependence.

Understanding dependent origination is like awakening to the symphony of the universe, where each note contributes to the melody of existence. It fosters a profound realization of the interconnectedness of all beings, cultivating compassion, empathy, and a sense of responsibility toward others and the world.

In exploring the nature of reality, the Bardo Thödol guides us along the Middle Way, a path that transcends the extremes of eternalism and nihilism. It teaches that reality is neither solely material nor solely spiritual, neither completely existent nor utterly non-existent. The Middle Way is the harmonious balance of understanding both the relative and absolute truths of existence.

Walking this path, we learn to embrace the paradoxes of life, to see beyond the dualities of pleasure and pain, gain and loss. It is a journey of awakening to the intrinsic freedom and luminosity of the mind, realizing that the nature of reality is a radiant emptiness, full of potentiality and possibilities.

One of the crowning jewels of the Bardo Thödol is the revelation of the luminous nature of the mind. The text elucidates that the essence of the mind is clear, unconditioned, and innately aware. This luminosity is not an external light but the inherent radiance of awareness, the innate wisdom that illuminates the path to enlightenment.

By recognizing and abiding in this innate awareness, practitioners can cut through the veil of ignorance, dispel the darkness of delusion, and awaken to their true nature. The realization of the luminous mind is the gateway to liberation, the key to unlocking the mysteries of existence and the ultimate truth of reality.

The Mind: Its Essence and Function

The Bardo Thödol introduces us to the mind's inherent luminosity, a radiant clarity untarnished by the transient play of thoughts and emotions. This luminous nature is not an acquired quality, but the mind's primordial state – clear, boundless, and infinitely compassionate. The text guides us to recognize this intrinsic purity, inviting us to rest in the luminous expanse of awareness and experience the union of wisdom and compassion.

Venturing further, we discover the mind as a ceaseless creator, shaping realms of existence with the brushstrokes of thoughts, desires, and karmic imprints. The Bardo Thödol illuminates the mind's creative potency, revealing how our perceptions, beliefs, and actions craft the tapestry of our reality. Understanding this, we learn to navigate the mind's landscapes with wisdom, cultivating virtuous thoughts and compassionate actions, shaping a harmonious and enlightened existence.

Within the mind's vast expanse, thoughts and emotions dance like fleeting clouds across the sky. The Bardo Thödol teaches us to witness this dance with equanimity, neither clinging to the pleasant nor recoiling from the unpleasant. By observing the transient nature of mental phenomena, we cultivate detachment and discernment, realizing the liberation inherent in every moment.

The journey through the Bardo Thödol is enriched by the practices of mindfulness and meditation. These practices are not mere techniques but portals into the depth of the mind, fostering awareness, tranquility, and insight. The text offers a myriad of meditation practices, each a golden key unlocking the treasures of the mind, guiding us towards the realization of our inherent wisdom and compassion.

In the sacred teachings of the Bardo Thödol, the mind's transformation is an alchemical process, a journey from the lead of ignorance to the gold of enlightenment. The text provides us with the tools and teachings for this inner alchemy, guiding us through the fires of purification, the waters of reflection, and the winds of realization. By embracing this alchemical journey, we transmute the base elements of the mind into the luminous gold of wisdom and compassion.

The Interplay between Mind and Reality

As we've unearthed, the mind in the Bardo Thödol is depicted as a powerful creator, a malleable force that sculpts our perceived reality. It is through the mind's creative potency that the world around us takes form, shaped by the colors of our thoughts, the textures of our emotions, and the shadows of our desires. Here, we delve deeper into understanding how this creative process functions, influencing not only our individual experiences but also the collective tapestry of existence.

The teachings of the Bardo Thödol elucidate the mind's role in perceiving and projecting reality. Our perceptions are not mere reflections of an objective world but are imbued with the hues of our subjective experiences. The mind projects its inner landscapes onto the canvas of the external world, coloring it with the shades of our hopes, fears, and aspirations. This section explores the dynamic of perception and projection, guiding us to discern the interweaving of the inner and outer, the subjective and objective.

The concept of karma is pivotal in understanding the interplay between mind and reality. Karma, in the teachings of the Bardo Thödol, is the invisible thread that connects our thoughts, words, and actions with the experiences they generate. It is the law of cause and effect playing out in the theater of existence, linking the mind with the unfolding of reality. We'll explore the intricacies of karmic connections and how they shape our journey through life, death, and rebirth.

A central theme in the Bardo Thödol is the recognition of the illusory nature of both the mind and the reality it perceives. By realizing that what we perceive as solid and real is, in fact, a dance of transient and interdependent phenomena, we unlock the door to liberation. This section delves into the liberating power of recognizing illusion, guiding us towards a deeper understanding of the ephemeral and the eternal.

As we navigate the interplay between mind and reality, the Bardo Thödol teaches us to embrace this dance with wisdom and compassion. It is not a path of renunciation but of engagement, not of escape but of immersion. By fully participating in the dance of existence, by recognizing the mind's creative role and the illusory nature of reality, we find the path to liberation and enlightenment.

Impermanence and Transience

As the winds of the Himalayas whisk through the mountainous terrains, carrying whispers of ancient wisdom, the Bardo Thödol unfolds a profound truth—one that defines the essence of our existence and the cosmos. This truth is the transient nature of all phenomena, a concept that the Tibetan Book of the Dead delicately yet unmistakably imprints on the canvas of our understanding.

Impermanence, as elucidated by the Bardo Thödol, is not just a philosophical concept but the very fabric of existence. It's the gentle hum of the river, the fleeting dance of the shadows, the ephemeral bloom of the flowers—it's the transient symphony that composes the melody of life.

Understanding impermanence is not to embrace pessimism, but to awaken to the richness of the present moment. It's to realize that every moment is unique, unrepeatable, and invaluable. It's to appreciate the beauty in transience, to find joy in the ephemeral dance of existence, and to live with a heart open to the ever-changing symphony of life.

The teachings of the Bardo Thödol invite us to observe the world with eyes unclouded by attachment and aversion. We begin to see that all forms and phenomena are fluid, ever-changing, and devoid of inherent permanence. Mountains erode, rivers change their course, and the stars in the night sky are in a perpetual dance of transformation.

This realization cultivates a sense of liberation and equanimity. We learn to let go of our rigid attachments, to flow with the currents of change, and to embrace the impermanent nature of the world with grace and wisdom. The fluidity of form and phenomena becomes a teacher, guiding us toward a deeper understanding of the transient nature of existence.

In the heart of transience, we find the wisdom of non-attachment. The Bardo Thödol teaches that by understanding and embracing impermanence, we naturally cultivate non-attachment. We no longer cling to the fleeting pleasures of the world, nor do we recoil from its transient pains. We walk the path of life with a balanced heart, appreciating the beauty of each moment without becoming ensnared by it.

This wisdom is not a withdrawal from the world but a deeper engagement with it. It's a celebration of the transient beauty of life, a dance with the ever-changing rhythms of existence. Non-attachment, as taught by the Bardo Thödol, is the gateway to true freedom, the foundation of compassion, and the wellspring of authentic joy.

The teachings on impermanence and transience are not meant to induce fear or despair, but to illuminate the path to liberation. By embracing change, by dancing with the transient rhythms of life, we awaken to the impermanence of all phenomena and the possibility of liberation from the cycle of birth and death.

The Bardo Thödol invites us to live fully, to love deeply, and to let go gracefully. It guides us to find peace in impermanence, wisdom in transience, and liberation in every breath. In the dance of impermanence, in the symphony of change, we find the melody of liberation and the harmony of enlightened existence.

Samsara: The Cycle of Birth, Death, and Rebirth

Samsara is often depicted as a wheel, a perpetual cycle where beings wander, driven by the winds of karma and delusion. The Bardo Thödol illuminates the intricate workings of this wheel, showcasing how beings are propelled through various realms of existence, experiencing the fruits of their actions and the ever-changing landscapes of joy and suffering.

Within the wheel of Samsara, the Bardo Thödol outlines six realms—each a manifestation of distinct mental states and karmic consequences. From the blissful heavens of the gods to the tormented hells, we explore each realm, understanding the experiences that inhabit them and the lessons they hold for the wanderer.

Deva Realm (Gods)
In the heavenly spheres of the Deva Realm, beings experience unparalleled bliss, pleasure, and longevity. However, despite such divine ecstasy and celestial abundance, the Bardo Thödol elucidates that this bliss is impermanent and can foster attachment and complacency, leading to spiritual stagnation and eventual fall into lower realms as the merit that brought them there is exhausted.

Asura Realm (Jealous Gods)
The Asuras, while experiencing considerable pleasure, are constantly plagued by envy towards the Devas, leading to conflict and struggle. The Bardo Thödol teaches that the root of suffering in this realm is jealousy and competitive striving, and the path to liberation lies in cultivating contentment and compassion.

Human Realm
Considered the most favorable for spiritual practice, the Human Realm provides a balance of pleasure and pain, fostering conditions for empathy, moral reflection, and the pursuit of enlightenment. The teachings of the Bardo Thödol

emphasize the precious opportunity this realm presents for spiritual growth and attainment of wisdom.

Animal Realm

Characterized by instinct, ignorance, and vulnerability, beings in the Animal Realm are subject to predation, hunger, and fear. The Bardo Thödol encourages the cultivation of awareness and kindness to transcend the limitations of this realm and progress towards higher states of being.

Preta Realm (Hungry Ghosts)

The tormented denizens of the Preta Realm are unable to satisfy their insatiable cravings, symbolizing the suffering of attachment and unfulfilled desires. The Bardo Thödol highlights the importance of generosity and detachment to overcome the afflictions of this realm.

Naraka Realm (Hells)

A place of intense suffering and purification, the Naraka Realm sees beings undergoing the consequences of harmful actions. Despite the severity of suffering, the Bardo Thödol teaches that this realm is not eternal, and through the exhaustion of negative karma and cultivation of virtue, beings can ascend to higher realms.

Karma, the law of moral causation, stands as the unseen architect of Samsara, shaping the destinies of beings and crafting the worlds they inhabit. The Bardo Thödol doesn't merely depict the entrapment within Samsara; it also illuminates the path to liberation. By cultivating wisdom, compassion, and ethical conduct, and by realizing the true nature of reality, beings can break the chains of karma, transcend the cycle of Samsara, and attain the ultimate freedom of enlightenment.

Amidst the teachings on liberation, the Bardo Thödol celebrates the Bodhisattva Ideal—the aspiration to attain enlightenment for the benefit of all sentient beings.

Liberation through Understanding

The Bardo Thödol beckons us to unlock the gates of perception and peer into the myriad realms of existence. It guides us to see beyond the veils of illusion, to dismantle the constructs of the mind, and to gaze upon the luminous nature of reality. Each verse, each syllable, is a key, unlocking profound insights and illuminating the path to liberation.

Understanding, in the context of the Bardo Thödol, is an awakening. It's a gentle unfolding of the petals of awareness, revealing the radiant heart of wisdom that resides within. It's a journey of discovery, where each step is a dance with the divine, each breath a hymn of enlightenment.

As we delve deeper into the wisdom of the Bardo Thödol, we are introduced to the mirror of mindfulness—a reflective pool of awareness that reveals the true nature of the self and the cosmos. Here, thoughts, emotions, and perceptions are seen as transient waves, arising and subsiding in the vast ocean of consciousness.

Mindfulness, as elucidated in the text, is not a passive observation but an active engagement with the present moment. It's a cultivation of discernment, a refinement of awareness, and a harmonization of mind and heart. Through the practice of mindfulness, we become the sovereigns of our inner realms, navigating the waters of existence with grace and wisdom.

The Bardo Thödol paints a cosmic dance of emptiness and form, where the phenomenal world is a divine play of the absolute. Understanding this dance is to realize the inseparability of emptiness and form, to see the divine in the mundane, and to recognize the sacredness of all existence.

Embracing this wisdom, we no longer perceive the world as a mere collection of separate entities but as a harmonious whole—a symphony of interconnectedness, a tapestry of interbeing. This realization is a gateway to compassion, a foundation for ethical conduct, and a wellspring of boundless love.

Liberation through understanding is the alchemy of transformation—a sacred process where the lead of ignorance is transmuted into the gold of wisdom. The Bardo Thödol is a master alchemist, guiding us through the fires of purification, the waters of reflection, and the winds of realization.

The Four Noble Truths

In the Bardo Thödol, the Four Noble Truths are intricately woven, serving as the cornerstone of its teachings and the compass guiding practitioners through the labyrinth of life, death, and rebirth. These truths, fundamental to Buddhist philosophy, are not explicitly laid out in a structured manner within the text; instead, they are embedded in its verses, shimmering through the allegories and vivid depictions of the bardos.

The First Noble Truth: Dukkha – The Nature of Suffering
Delve into the profundity of the first noble truth, Dukkha, as the Bardo Thödol paints a vivid picture of the inherent suffering that permeates existence. By acknowledging the omnipresence of suffering, we unveil the curtain to a deeper understanding of the human condition and the transient nature of the material world.

The Second Noble Truth: Samudaya – The Origin of Suffering
With a discerning eye, we explore Samudaya, unravelling the roots of suffering. The Bardo Thödol provides insight into the intertwining desires, aversions, and ignorance that fuel the cycle of suffering, granting us the clarity to discern the chains that bind us to the wheel of Samsara.

The Third Noble Truth: Nirodha – The Cessation of Suffering

Discover the realm of possibilities as the Bardo Thödol illuminates Nirodha, the cessation of suffering. Here, we explore the potential for liberation, the extinguishing of the flames of desire, and the attainment of Nirvana – the ultimate state of peace and unconditioned freedom.

The Fourth Noble Truth: Magga – The Path to Cessation
Guided by the wisdom of the Bardo Thödol, we traverse Magga, the path leading to the cessation of suffering. This section outlines the practical steps and ethical guidelines, the cultivation of wisdom and compassion, and the meditative practices that form the roadway to liberation.

The Eightfold Path

The Eightfold Path is a comprehensive guide to ethical living, mental cultivation, and profound wisdom. With each step, we uncover the timeless principles that illuminate the journey through life, death, and beyond, guiding the wayfarer toward the ultimate destination of enlightenment.

Right Understanding: Seeing the World with Clarity
Dive into the essence of perceiving the world through wisdom and truth. Cultivate discernment by recognizing the transient nature of existence, the interdependence of all beings, and the intrinsic reality that shapes our experiences.

Right Intention: Cultivating a Compassionate Heart
Nurture the seeds of compassion, love, and altruism. With a heart attuned to the well-being of others, we can foster harmonious relationships, dissolve the barriers of self-centeredness, and embrace the interconnectedness of all life.

Right Speech: The Harmonious Melody of Words
Step into the harmonious realm of mindful communication. Express truth with kindness, fostering understanding and creating an atmosphere of trust and mutual respect.

Right Action: Walking the Path of Virtue
Illuminate the ethical guidelines that guide our conduct. Navigate life's complexities with mindfulness and integrity, embodying non-harm, generosity, and moral purity.

Right Livelihood: Aligning Work with Ethical Principles
Discover the essence of aligning work with ethical principles, contributing to societal well-being, and fostering a sense of purpose and fulfillment.

Right Effort: Cultivating Positive Qualities
Delve into the energetic sphere where one is inspired to cultivate wholesome qualities, overcome negative tendencies, and nurture enlightenment within our hearts and minds.

Right Mindfulness: The Art of Present-Moment Awareness
Engage in the practice of cultivating present-moment awareness. Observe the ever-changing flow of experience and develop insight into the nature of reality.

Right Concentration: Focused Meditation and Spiritual Insight
Embark on a meditative journey to develop focused attention, cultivate inner tranquility, and experience the transformative power of spiritual insight.

Bodhicitta: Cultivating the Enlightened Mind

In the sacred teachings of the Bardo Thödol, Bodhicitta is described as the enlightened mind, the awakening heart that radiates boundless love and compassion towards all sentient beings. Here, we explore the practices and meditations that nurture this compassionate heart, fostering a deep sense of interconnectedness and a commitment to alleviating suffering in the world.

Delve into the profound dimensions of Bodhicitta, exploring its two inseparable aspects: relative and absolute. The relative aspect involves the cultivation of love, compassion, and the aspiration to attain enlightenment for the benefit of others, while the absolute aspect is the direct realization of the ultimate nature of reality, beyond concepts and dualities.

Learn about the significance of generating an altruistic intention in the cultivation of Bodhicitta. The Bardo Thödol emphasizes the importance of developing a sincere aspiration to attain enlightenment for the sake of others, thereby transforming every thought, word, and action into a means of benefiting sentient beings.

Bodhicitta teaches us to embrace life's challenges as opportunities for spiritual growth and transformation. This section explores how the teachings of the Bardo Thödol guide practitioners in transforming adversity into wisdom, utilizing obstacles as catalysts for developing patience, compassion, and a deeper understanding of the human experience.

The Six Perfections: Perfecting Virtue

The Six Perfections (Paramitas) is a core teaching of Mahayana Buddhism beautifully encapsulated within the teachings of the Bardo Thödol. These six virtues form the foundation for cultivating a compassionate and enlightened mind, guiding practitioners along the path to Buddhahood.

1. Generosity (Dāna): The Joy of Giving
As the first perfection, Generosity uncovers the multifaceted nature of giving. Delve into the forms of generosity—giving of material resources, protection from fear, and spiritual guidance—and understand how this selfless practice nurtures an open heart and diminishes attachment and greed.

2. Ethical Conduct (Śīla): Living in Harmony

The essence of Ethical Conduct, the second perfection, and learn how living by ethical principles fosters harmony with oneself, others, and the environment. Examine the five precepts and the importance of non-harming, honesty, and moral integrity on the spiritual path.

3. Patience (Kṣānti): Embracing Equanimity

The transformative power of Patience, the third perfection. Understand the various forms of patience—tolerating harm, enduring suffering, and accepting the truth—and learn how cultivating patience leads to inner peace, resilience, and a deeper understanding of the impermanence of life.

4. Diligence (Vīrya): Cultivating Joyful Effort

Immerse yourself in the teachings on Diligence, the fourth perfection, and explore how joyful effort and unwavering dedication fuel spiritual progress. Discover the balance between effort and ease, and learn practical methods to overcome laziness, procrastination, and discouragement.

5. Concentration (Dhyāna): Mastering the Mind

Delve into the world of Concentration, the fifth perfection, and understand its pivotal role in mastering the mind and cultivating insight. Learn various meditation techniques, the importance of mindfulness and single-pointed focus, and the path to achieving meditative absorption and tranquility.

6. Wisdom (Prajñā): Realizing Ultimate Truth

Embark on the exploration of Wisdom, the sixth and final perfection, and uncover the profound teachings on the nature of reality, emptiness, and interdependence. Realize the importance of wisdom in dispelling ignorance and delusion and discover how this ultimate understanding leads to liberation and enlightenment.

Vajrayana Practices and Dzogchen

Within the boundless wisdom of the Bardo Thödol, the paths of Vajrayana and Dzogchen are revealed as advanced and profound methodologies for spiritual enlightenment. This chapter unveils these intricate paths, elucidating the esoteric practices, mystical philosophies, and transformative experiences that characterize Vajrayana and Dzogchen.

Vajrayana, the Diamond Vehicle, introduces us to the realm of tantric mysticism. Here, we examine its emphasis on ritual, symbolism, and inner transformation. We delve into the practice of deity yoga, the use of mandalas and mantras, and the role of empowerment in initiating practitioners into tantric practices.

Dzogchen, known as the Great Perfection, stands as the pinnacle of spiritual realization within the Nyingma school of Tibetan Buddhism. This section illuminates the essence of Dzogchen, revealing its teachings on the natural state of mind, spontaneous presence, and the direct experience of enlightenment within every moment.

Uncover the synergistic union of method and wisdom within Vajrayana and Dzogchen practices. This union harmoniously integrates compassion and emptiness, skillful means and insight, leading practitioners to the realization of the non-dual nature of reality and the manifestation of enlightened activities.

Vajrayana and Dzogchen emphasize the integration of spiritual practice into the fabric of everyday life. We explore how practitioners apply mindfulness, visualization, and contemplation in daily activities, transforming ordinary experiences into opportunities for awakening and cultivating a seamless continuity of awareness.

The relationship with a spiritual teacher or guru holds paramount importance in both Vajrayana and Dzogchen. Here, we discuss the qualities of a genuine guru, the dynamics of guru-disciple relationships, and the significance of receiving transmissions and teachings that illuminate the path to enlightenment.

Chapter Nine

Influence on Western Thought and Popular Culture

Early Western Encounters

When we look into the first interactions between the esoteric teachings of the Bardo Thödol and the explorative minds of the Western world, we find ourselves amidst a confluence of curiosity, skepticism, and revelation. The air is charged with the allure of the unknown and the possibility of bridging disparate worlds.

Delving into the annals of history, we stumble upon the advent of Western explorers and scholars setting foot on the high plateaus of Tibet. The landscape, as untamed as the knowledge it concealed, promised a treasure trove of ancient wisdom. It was amidst these craggy terrains and misty monasteries that the Bardo Thödol was first discovered by the Western intellect. The task of translating such a profound text was no easy feat—it required a harmonious marriage of linguistic proficiency and philosophical insight, a delicate dance between staying true to the essence and making it accessible to unfamiliar minds.

The early translations of the Bardo Thödol brought forth a cascade of inter-pretations, each unveiling a different facet of the diamond. Scholars and spiritual seekers alike found themselves enamored by the vivid imagery, the profound philosophy, and the intricate rituals. However, the journey through this spiritual landscape was not without its pitfalls. The Western lens, often tinted with its own cultural, religious, and philosophical biases, sometimes distorted the orig-inal teachings, leading to misinterpretations and oversimplifications. Yet, these very challenges fueled a deeper quest for understanding and a refinement of the interpretive process.

The ripples of the Bardo Thödol's teachings did not merely stay confined to the academic and spiritual circles—they permeated into the fabric of Western thought, philosophy, and psychology. Pioneers such as Carl Jung found reso-nance with the text's exploration of the human psyche, and the Bardo Thödol served as a bridge between Eastern and Western notions of consciousness, life, death, and rebirth. The text ignited conversations around the nature of reality, the mind, and the potential for transformation and liberation, contributing to a cross-cultural dialogue and spiritual synthesis.

As the Bardo Thödol continued to seep into the consciousness of the West, it paved the way for a blossoming of cultural exchange and mutual enrichment. Western seekers journeyed to the East, immersing themselves in the practices and teachings of Tibetan Buddhism, while Eastern masters brought the light of Dharma to the Western shores. This exchange was not a one-way street—it was a dynamic interplay that saw both traditions learning, evolving, and enriching one another. The Bardo Thödol stood as a testament to the universal quest for truth and the capacity of the human spirit to transcend boundaries and unite in wisdom.

Influence on Western Philosophers and Psychologists

Exploring the impact of the Bardo Thödol on Western thought, we discover a rich blend of ancient wisdom and modern perspectives. Within the esteemed realms of philosophy and the complex pathways of psychology, the teachings of the Tibetan Book of the Dead have taken root, inspiring transformative ideas and sparking enlightening discussions.

Carl Jung, a titan in the realm of psychology, was among the first to embrace the profundities of the Bardo Thödol. With a mind attuned to the depths of the unconscious and the archetypes that dwell therein, Jung found in the ancient Tibetan text a mirror reflecting the universal journey of the soul. The Bardo Thödol's vivid depictions of the afterlife and the transformative states of consciousness resonated with Jung's theories of individuation and the collective unconscious, offering a harmonious symphony of Eastern wisdom and Western psychological thought.

Aldous Huxley, a luminary in literature and philosophy, was also deeply influenced by the teachings encapsulated within the Bardo Thödol. The text became a key that unlocked the doors of perception for Huxley, inspiring his exploration of altered states of consciousness and the nature of reality. Huxley's fascination with the Bardo Thödol found expression in his writings, weaving together threads of existential inquiry, spiritual awakening, and the human condition.

The arrival of the Bardo Thödol on Western shores ignited a confluence of philosophical dialogues, sparking conversations around life, death, rebirth, and the nature of existence. Philosophers found in its pages a rich reservoir of metaphysical insights and ethical guidelines, prompting reflections on the interconnectedness of all beings and the transient nature of the material world. The text inspired a spiritual synthesis, bridging Eastern and Western worldviews and contributing to a more holistic understanding of the human experience.

The influence rippled beyond the early pioneers, permeating the fields of integrative psychology and transpersonal studies. Scholars and practitioners explored the therapeutic applications of its teachings, incorporating meditation, mindfulness, and compassion-based approaches into psychological practice. The text's emphasis on the transformative potential of the mind and the journey towards enlightenment offered a fresh perspective on healing, well-being, and human potential.

The "Bardo Thödol" in Popular Culture, Literature, Art and Modern Media

In the embrace of creative minds, the wisdom of the Bardo Thödol has blossomed into a myriad of forms, enriching the world of literature and art. The text's profound teachings on life, death, and rebirth have inspired writers and artists, serving as a wellspring of thematic depth and aesthetic nuance.

Renowned authors have been captivated by the mystical allure of the Bardo Thödol, weaving its themes into the fabric of their narratives. The exploration of the afterlife, the transient nature of existence, and the pursuit of enlightenment have found resonance in novels, poems, and essays, offering readers a literary journey through the landscapes of the human soul and the cosmic order.

Aldous Huxley's "Island" is a prime example, portraying a utopian society where the inhabitants practice mindfulness and self-awareness, echoing the Bardo Thödol's teachings on the nature of mind and reality. Jack Kerouac's "The Dharma Bums" blends the spontaneity of the Beat Generation with the quest for enlightenment, drawing parallels with the journey outlined in the ancient Tibetan text.

In the realm of visual art, the Bardo Thödol's vibrant imagery and symbolism have inspired renowned artists like Salvador Dalí, whose surrealistic paintings often explore themes of impermanence and transformation, reminiscent of the transitional states described in the text. Yoko Ono's installations, emphasizing participatory and experiential art, reflect the text's focus on individual perception and experience of reality.

The text's vivid descriptions of the bardos have been translated into moving visuals by filmmakers such as Christopher Nolan in "Inception", where the concept of layered realities and the transient nature of life echo the teachings of the Bardo Thödol. Darren Aronofsky's "The Fountain" similarly explores themes of death, rebirth, and the quest for immortality, reflecting the cyclical nature of existence described in the ancient text.

Musically, the teachings of the Bardo Thödol have reverberated through the compositions of artists like George Harrison of The Beatles, whose exploration of Eastern spirituality in his music often drew from the themes of enlightenment and liberation found in the text. The psychedelic rock band The Doors, named after Aldous Huxley's book "The Doors of Perception", also incorporated themes inspired by Eastern spirituality, exploring perceptions of reality and consciousness.

With the advent of digital communication, the Bardo Thödol has found its voice in the conversations resonating through the vast expanse of podcasts and social media. Influencers, spiritual teachers, and curious minds alike have delved into its teachings, sparking discussions on life, death, and the afterlife, and sharing snippets of wisdom with followers from all walks of life. The digital realm has become a modern-day sangha, a community where seekers gather to explore and contemplate the teachings of the Bardo Thödol.

In today's popular culture and the buzzing world of modern media, the Bardo Thödol has found unexpected yet fertile ground to blossom and resonate with a diverse, global audience. Its ancient teachings have been reimagined and reincarnated through various mediums, striking a chord with individuals seeking meaning and connection in a fast-paced, ever-evolving world.

Integration into Western Spirituality

One of the significant contributions of the Bardo Thödol to Western spirituality has been the widespread adoption of mindfulness and meditation practices. The text's profound teachings on the nature of the mind and the cultivation of awareness have inspired countless individuals to embark on journeys of inner exploration and self-discovery. Meditation centers, retreats, and online platforms have flourished, fostering communities dedicated to practicing and living the wisdom of the Bardo Thödol.

The Bardo Thödol has played role in shaping the death positivity movement in the West. The text's portrayal of death as a transformative experience and an opportunity for spiritual awakening has challenged societal norms and encouraged open conversations about death, dying, and bereavement. This shift in perspective has led to the emergence of death cafes, end-of-life doulas, and holistic approaches to palliative care, reflecting the influence of the Bardo Thödol's teachings.

The arrival of the Bardo Thödol in the West has also fostered interfaith dialogues, bridging the gap between Eastern and Western spiritual traditions. These dialogues have facilitated mutual respect, understanding, and appreciation for the diversity of spiritual practices and beliefs. The Bardo Thödol's teachings have found common ground with various religious philosophies, contributing to shared wisdom and spiritual exploration.

The teachings on interdependence, impermanence, and compassion have found resonance with the eco-spirituality movement. The text has inspired environmental activists and spiritual practitioners to cultivate a deeper connection with the Earth and all living beings, fostering a sense of responsibility and a commitment to ecological sustainability and ethical living.

Chapter Ten

The Tibetan Book of the Dead and Science

Near-Death Experiences

Using the Bardo Thödol as a guide, we find parallels in how modern science approaches death. Once seen as a definite end, it's now viewed as a complex series of processes, aligning with the teachings of the Bardo Thödol.

The dance of life and death, depicted in the text as an intricate interplay of energies, finds its counterpart in the scientific exploration of cellular apoptosis and neurodegeneration. Here, the dissolution of the elements, as described in the ancient scripture, invites reflection on the molecular and physiological transformations that characterize the dying process.

The realm of near-death experiences (NDEs) offers a fascinating intersection where the narratives of the Bardo Thödol and empirical observations intertwine.

A figure of renown in the field of NDE research, Dr. Raymond A. Moody, with his seminal work, "Life After Life" (1975), catalyzed the scientific exploration of these extraordinary experiences. His extensive interviews with individuals who have brushed with death revealed commonalities such as moving through a tunnel, encountering a light, and feeling a sense of peace, which resonated with the Bardo Thödol's narrative of navigating through different bardos.

In 2001, the Lancet published a groundbreaking study led by Dutch cardiologist Dr. Pim van Lommel. This study scrutinized the NDEs of cardiac arrest survivors and proposed that such experiences could not be solely attributed to physiological processes. The findings ignited discussions on the nature of consciousness and its existence beyond the confines of the brain, inviting reflections on the Bardo Thödol's teachings about the mind and the afterlife.

Dr. Bruce Greyson, a prominent psychiatrist, has dedicated his career to examining the long-term effects of NDEs on individuals' lives. His research unveils transformative shifts in values, beliefs, and attitudes, aligning with the Bardo Thödol's depiction of the afterlife as a realm of profound insight and spiritual awakening.

The AWARE (AWAreness during REsuscitation) study, led by Dr. Sam Parnia, ventured into uncharted territories by investigating the veridical perceptions and awareness reported by cardiac arrest survivors during the time of their clinical death. This study adds a layer of depth to our understanding of consciousness during the dying process, resonating with the transitional states explored in the Bardo Thödol.

In all these studies individuals recounting their NDEs often speak of traversing through tunnels of light, encountering ethereal beings, and undergoing life reviews, motifs that resonate with the journey through various bardos.

The phenomenological richness of NDEs echoes the Bardo Thödol's vivid descriptions, inviting us to explore the boundaries of consciousness and the nature of subjective reality. The confluence of these experiences fosters a dialogue that transcends temporal and cultural divides, bridging the ancient and the modern, the mystical and the empirical.

This exploration of NDEs through the prism of the Bardo Thödol illuminates the potential for interdisciplinary inquiry, shedding light on the universality of certain experiences and the diverse cultural lenses through which they are interpreted.

The concept of reincarnation is a golden thread woven through the fabric of the Bardo Thödol, depicting the cyclical nature of existence and the continuum of consciousness. Scientific curiosity around this ancient belief has given rise to a body of research examining cases suggestive of past-life memories, particularly among children.

Psychology and Mental States

In the labyrinth of the human psyche, Carl Jung discovered the mysterious realm of the Collective Unconscious, where archetypal imagery and mythic narratives reside. These universal symbols, according to Jung, are the shared heritage of humanity, imprinted in the depths of our psyche. When we delve into the vivid imagery and transformative narratives of the Bardo Thödol, we find an intriguing resonance with Jung's theories, offering a bridge between the ancient wisdom of Tibetan Buddhism and the modern insights of depth psychology.

The Bardo Thödol paints a kaleidoscopic canvas of deities, demons, and landscapes, each symbolizing aspects of the human psyche and the spiritual journey. These images, though culturally and historically rooted in Tibetan Buddhism, bear a striking resemblance to the archetypes identified by Jung. The wrathful and peaceful deities encountered in the bardos can be seen as manifestations of our innermost fears, desires, and potentials, offering a mirror to reflect upon our own mental states.

Carl Jung was profoundly influenced by the Bardo Thödol, seeing in its teachings a confirmation of his own ideas about the psyche's inner workings. He perceived the bardo experiences as representative of the individuation process – the journey towards wholeness and self-realization. The intricate dance between the ego and the Self, between light and shadow, finds a poetic expression in the Bardo Thödol's narratives, inviting readers to confront and integrate the disparate aspects of their being.

For Jung, the Bardo Thödol was not just a guide to the afterlife, but a manual for the living, a tool for psychological transformation. He saw the potential for the teachings of the Bardo Thödol to facilitate a deep exploration of the unconscious, enabling individuals to uncover hidden aspects of their psyche and achieve greater self-awareness. The dialogues with deities and demons in the bardos become inner dialogues, opportunities for introspection and growth.

In the interplay between the Bardo Thödol and Jungian psychology, we find insights into the human mind. The archetypal imagery and transformative narratives of the Bardo Thödol provide a gateway to the Collective Unconscious, where ancient wisdom and modern psychology converge. This synthesis invites us to embark on a journey of self-discovery, to embrace the mysteries of the psyche, and to explore the boundless landscapes of the mind.

As we traverse the realms of the Bardo Thödol and the depths of the unconscious, we are guided by the light of ancient wisdom and the torch of scientific inquiry. The dance between psychology and spirituality, between science and mysticism, reveals the multifaceted nature of the human experience, inviting us to delve deeper, to question further, and to embrace the complexity of our being. In the embrace of archetypal imagery and psychological insight, the Bardo Thödol becomes a compass for the soul, guiding us through the uncharted territories of the mind and the vast expanse of the human spirit.

Neuroscience and Brain Studies

The serenity of meditation and the bustling activity of the brain may seem like opposing phenomena, yet they converge in a fascinating dance of neuroscience. The ancient practice of meditation, deeply embedded in the teachings of the

Bardo Thödol, finds a contemporary counterpart in the rigor of neuroimaging studies. Scientists, armed with advanced technologies like fMRI and EEG, have embarked on a journey to uncover the neural correlates of meditation, and the findings are nothing short of illuminating.

Meditators, both novice and seasoned, exhibit distinctive patterns of brain activity, revealing the profound impact of meditation on neural networks. The prefrontal cortex, the seat of executive functions, shows enhanced connectivity, pointing towards improved attention and cognitive control. The amygdala, our emotion center, displays modulated activity, suggesting a refined emotional regulation. These alterations in brain activity not only substantiate the transformative potential of meditation but also resonate with the mental states described in the Bardo Thödol.

Delving deeper, neuroimaging studies unveil the intricate dance between different brain regions during meditation. The default mode network, often associated with self-referential thinking and mind-wandering, exhibits decreased activity, indicative of a quieting of the mind. This neural quietude mirrors the tranquility and heightened awareness advocated by the Bardo Thödol, offering a glimpse into the neurological underpinnings of meditative states.

Venturing into the realms of consciousness, neuroscience seeks to unravel the mysteries of the mind, and in doing so, finds echoes of the insights from the Bardo Thödol. The exploration of brain states during death, dreaming, and meditation sheds light on the neural dynamics underlying the varied states of consciousness described in the ancient text.

Scientific investigations into near-death experiences and altered states of consciousness reveal intriguing parallels with the bardo states. The surge in brain activity at the brink of death, the vivid imagery, and the sense of transcending time and space all resonate with the narratives of the Bardo Thödol. These scientific observations invite contemplation on the nature of consciousness and the interconnectedness of life and death, enriching our understanding of the bardo experiences.

Moreover, the study of brain activity during dreaming and deep meditation uncovers the neural substrates of these altered states, providing a tangible link to the ephemeral experiences of the bardos. The oscillations between REM and non-REM sleep, the shifts in brainwave patterns, and the activation of specific neural circuits all paint a dynamic portrait of the dreaming brain, echoing the fluidity and vividness of the bardo states.

Quantum Physics and the Nature of Reality

The Bardo Thödol invites us on a profound journey through the multilayered realms of existence, where consciousness takes center stage in shaping our experiences. In a fascinating alignment with this ancient wisdom, quantum physics offers a tantalizing glimpse into the nature of reality, where particles can exist in multiple states and locations simultaneously. Could the teachings of the Bardo Thödol be subtly hinting at a quantum interpretation of reality?

This intersection between ancient wisdom and cutting-edge science invites us to reconsider the fabric of reality itself. The Bardo Thödol's depictions of various bardos—transitional states of existence—echo the quantum realm's elusive and dynamic nature. Here, consciousness is not a mere observer; it is an active participant, entangled with the world it perceives. The myriad possibilities presented in the quantum realm mirror the Bardo Thödol's teachings on the fluidity and malleability of our experiences in the bardos.

One of the cornerstone principles of quantum physics is entanglement, a phenomenon where particles, once interacted, remain connected regardless of the distance separating them. A change in the state of one particle instantaneously affects the state of the other, transcending the limitations of space and time. This non-locality challenges our conventional understanding of the universe and offers a compelling reflection on interconnectedness.

The Bardo Thödol, too, speaks of a deep interconnectedness that permeates all of existence. It teaches that our actions, thoughts, and intentions ripple through the fabric of reality, shaping our experiences and influencing the world around us. This interconnectedness aligns with the quantum principle of entanglement, suggesting a harmonious dance between individual consciousness and the collective whole.

As we traverse the bridges between the Bardo Thödol's ancient wisdom and the revelations of quantum physics, we uncover insights that illuminate our understanding of reality. The multidimensional realms depicted in the Bardo Thödol find resonance with the quantum landscape, where particles dance in a symphony of possibilities, and the universe reveals its interconnected nature.

This harmonious interplay between ancient teachings and modern science beckons us to explore further, to question deeper, and to embrace the mysteries of existence. The Bardo Thödol, with its rich narratives and profound teachings, invites us to look beyond the veil of the material world and glimpse the infinite possibilities that lie within the quantum canvas of reality.

Integrative Approaches and Future Directions

The wisdom of the Bardo Thödol, combined with modern scientific discoveries, presents a comprehensive understanding. Insights from the ancient Tibetan text merge seamlessly with those from neuroscience, quantum physics, and psychology, highlighting the connections between these varied fields.

Opportunities for integrative research abound, beckoning scholars and spiritual practitioners alike to transcend disciplinary boundaries and embark on a quest for unified wisdom. The rich imagery and profound teachings of the Bardo Thödol offer fertile ground for exploring the depths of the human psyche, the nature of consciousness, and the mysteries of existence. At the same time, advancements in scientific methodologies and technologies provide the tools to probe, quantify, and analyze these realms, bridging the gap between the subjective and objective, the experiential and the empirical.

This confluence of ancient wisdom and contemporary science opens avenues for multidisciplinary collaborations, fostering a dialogue that transcends the dichotomy between spirituality and science. Researchers and practitioners can delve into the exploration of meditative states, near-death experiences, and altered states of consciousness, drawing parallels between the narratives of the Bardo Thödol and empirical findings. Such integrative approaches hold the promise of enriching our understanding of the human condition, unveiling the intricate interplay between mind, body, and spirit, and illuminating the path towards holistic well-being.

Peering into the horizon, the landscape of integrative research on the Bardo Thödol and science is dotted with emerging trends and uncharted territories. The confluence of technological innovation and spiritual inquiry is giving rise to novel research paradigms, pushing the boundaries of what we know and beckoning us to explore the unknown.

One of the promising frontiers is the exploration of consciousness through the lens of quantum physics and neuroscience, delving into the mysteries of non-locality, entanglement, and the nature of reality. The multidimensional realities described in the Bardo Thödol find echoes in the quantum realm, inviting researchers to ponder the interconnectedness of all existence and the possibility of a unified field of consciousness.

Moreover, advancements in neuroimaging and brain-computer interfaces are enabling researchers to map the neural correlates of meditative states, near-death experiences, and altered states of consciousness with unprecedented precision. These technological breakthroughs offer a window into the mind, allowing us to visualize the ebb and flow of thoughts, emotions, and sensations, and to unravel the neural underpinnings of the bardo states.

As we venture into these uncharted territories, the Bardo Thödol serves as a compass, guiding us through the labyrinth of existence and inspiring us to seek deeper truths. The fusion of ancient teachings and modern science is forging a path towards a more holistic and integrated understanding of the human experience, opening the gates to a realm where wisdom and knowledge dance in harmonious unity.